THE HERITAGE OF THE BHIKKHU

OTHER BOOKS BY WALPOLA RĀHULA

Published by Grove Press

What the Buddha Taught

ALSO BY WALPOLA RĀHULA

History of Buddhism in Ceylon
Laṃkāvē Budusamayehi Itihāsaya
Budun Vadāḷa Dharmaya
Le Compendium de la Super-doctrine (*Abhidharma-samuccaya*) d'Asaṅga
(translator and annotator)

WALPOLA RĀHULA

THE HERITAGE OF THE BHIKKHU

A SHORT HISTORY OF THE BHIKKHU IN EDUCATIONAL, CULTURAL, SOCIAL, AND POLITICAL LIFE

FOREWORD BY EDMUND F. PERRY

TRANSLATED BY
K.P.G. WIJAYASURENDRA
AND REVISED BY THE AUTHOR

GROVE PRESS, INC. NEW YORK

ISBN: 0-394-49190-4
Grove ISBN: 0-8021-0012-0
Library of Congress Catalog Card Number: 73-19215

First Printing

Manufactured in the United States of America

Distributed by Random House, Inc.

GROVE PRESS, INC., 53 East 11th Street, New York, New York 10003

The Heritage of the Bhikkhu was originally published as *Bhikṣuvagē Urumaya* by Svastika Press, Colombo, 1946.

To the memory of those thousands,
bhikkhus and others,
who sacrificed their lives
in the political struggle in Ceylon
in 1971

CONTENTS

Foreword to the English Edition
by Edmund F. Perry xi
Author's Preface xvii
Introduction to the Second Sinhala Edition xix
Preface to the First Sinhala Edition xxv
Chronology xxvii
1. Buddhism and Social Service 3
2. The Evolution of the Life of the *Bhikkhu* 8
3. The Councils 13
4. Introduction of Buddhism to Ceylon: The National Religion of the Sinhala People 16
5. Religio-Nationalism and National Culture 20
6. Fundamental Innovations 24
7. Study and Meditation: Academic Developments 29
8. Monasteries: Their Administration and Maintenance 34
9. Arts, Crafts, and Literature 40
10. National Freedom and the Protection of Peace 50
11. The Portuguese Period 55
12. The Dutch Period 58
13. British Rule 63
14. Struggle for Freedom: Rebellions 66

15. The Strength of *Bhikkhus:* Lay-Clergy Unity 68
16. British Tactics: Disruption of Lay-Clergy Unity 71
17. British Tactics: Confusion of Monastic Administration 79
18. British Tactics: Intrigues to Destroy Buddhism (Christian Education) 82
19. National and Religious Degeneration 90
20. The Revival 93
Postscript 98
Appendix I. What is Politics? 120
Appendix II. *Bhikkhus* and Politics: Declaration of the Vidyālaṅkāra Pirivena 131
Appendix III. The Kälaṇiya Declaration of Independence (January 6, 1947) 134
Appendix IV. Basic Points Unifying the Theravāda and the Mahāyāna 137
Glossary of Terms 139
Notes 150
Bibliography 165
Index 168

ILLUSTRATIONS

The Ruvanväli-sāya at Anurādhapura 43

An assembly of *bhikkhus* 43

A *bhikkhu* addressing a mass meeting 44

Examining palm leaf manuscripts of the Pāli *Tipiṭaka* 44

A class of children learning Buddhism under a Bo tree 45

Vidyodaya University 45

Vidyālaṅkāra University 46

At the Independence Day Celebration in Kandy 44

Buddhist-Christian memorial service for the Rev. Dr. Martin Luther King 47

FOREWORD TO THE ENGLISH EDITION

By Edmund F. Perry,
Professor of the Comparative Study of Religions,
Northwestern University

This book presents a reliable account of the Buddhist monk's mode of life and his range of leadership responsibilities from the time of the Buddha to the insurgency in Ceylon in 1971. The publication of this book in English appears auspiciously at the very time when an entire generation of youth and Western scholars seek to know what the Asian religions offer to mankind. Interest in the identity of the Buddhist monk (*bhikkhu*) centers on his personal pursuit of perfection and his life as a type of public leader.

Bhikkhu Walpola Rāhula wrote *The Heritage of the Bhikkhu* during his own vigorous participation in the movement to gain Ceylon's independence from the British. He wrote the book to inform his own countrymen, Buddhist monks and laymen, of the role which the Buddhist tradition had formed for and bequeathed to the monk. This fascinating story discloses a genre of indefatigable men, in generation after generation, who disciplined their own lives, who taught others, and who served others in the total range of their individual, social, and spiritual needs. Bhikkhu Rāhula's account recalled to his countrymen that historically the Buddhist monk had participated in public affairs, including participation in political decision making and political action which affect the common welfare and possibility of happiness for the masses of people.

The image of the Buddhist monk as a public leader engaging in social and political activities had been obscured, deliberately so, by Western colonialists and their accompanying Christian missionaries. By imposing a particular type of Christian monasticism upon the Buddhist clergy, restricting the clergy's activity to individual purification and temple ministries, the colonial administrators dispossessed the *bhikkhus* of their influence on the public life of their people and actually succeeded in instituting a tradition of Buddhist recluses, to the near exclusion of other types of clergy.

Truth and Christian conviction, with the advantage of hindsight, compel me, who am myself an orthodox Christian, to call attention to the accuracy of Bhikkhu Rāhula's references to the complicity of many Christians in the colonial subjection of the Buddhists of Asia and in the suppression of their monks by shameful intrigues and deceits. The conspiracy to "convert" the Buddhist monk from public leader to disengaged recluse prevailed so widely and pervasively that today even in independent countries the monks have to struggle against so-called Buddhist politicians who, still possessed by the "heritage" left by the imperialists, want, more than the colonial Christians, to silence and seclude the monks as though the monk constitutes a public menace. Professor Rāhula has exposed this present-day political effort perpetrated against the monks by "professing" Buddhist politicians.

Western scholarship has failed to correct misrepresentations of the Buddhist monk. To this day Western scholars of Buddhism tend to perpetuate the image of the Buddhist monk as something like the medieval mystic recluse of the Christian faith. And certainly some Buddhists, lay as well as monastics, have withdrawn from society and sought individual perfection in solitariness. But, Professor Rāhula reminds us, Buddhism does not make a virtue of spiritual solitude. So, even as *The Heritage of the Bhikkhu* sought in its Sinhalese original to recover the distinctively Buddhist character and role of the monk, so now in its English translation and expanded edition it seeks to correct misrepresentations made by well-intentioned investigators from Western universities. Western students who have achieved a technical mastery of the languages of the Buddhists can translate literal or postulated, but rarely ever cultural, meanings for words in Buddhist texts or in usage by living Buddhists. Hence misrepresentations continue.

The Venerable Professor Rāhula recapitulates in his own mentality the culture of the Order of Buddhist Monks. Based upon his own heritage of the monk's culture and his own cultivation of incomparable competency in the languages, philosophy, and history of the *bhikkhu*, Professor Rāhula offers us an essay both easy to read and to understand. At the same time, the precise vocabulary and simplicity of expression which make this a fascinating and understandable essay also open up to us scholarly information and profound insights hitherto unknown outside of Buddhist countries and Asian languages.

Both the book, *The Heritage of the Bhikkhu,* and its author have now become a part of the *bhikkhu's* heritage, for Rāhula has formed his own life as a monk along the lines set in the classical tradition of Buddhism. At the time he was engaged in the Ceylon independence movement, Bhikkhu Rāhula was characterized in D. B. Dhanapala's *Eminent Indians* as "a scholar, an organizer, a planner, a preacher, a debater, a writer" and a champion of the people misled and misguided by the colonial colossus. He interrupted his career as a scholar to emancipate those Buddhist monks "confined to [their] temple and exploited by politicians at election time . . . denied modern education, cut off from the life of the people." He won over to his position the influential monastery, Vidyālaṅkāra Pirivena, and thereby, within weeks, the support of thousands of monks who, with him, inveighed against reactionary politicians.

He enheartened the masses of hungry people in the 1940's. Twenty years later he headed an institution of higher education in Ceylon, an institution which, as a coeductional university, betokened his vision of equal educational opportunity for every child born in Ceylon. Many of his students in this university were children of those masses he had inspired twenty or more years earlier. Rāhula planted in the children's minds the hope of a decent and economically self-sufficient Ceylon. If, as Dhanapala continued in *Eminent Indians,* Buddhist Ceylon was divided into two camps, "pro-Rāhula and anti-Rāhula," today it is equally so, but not because Rāhula is the issue, but because freedom, education, and economic security are issues synonymous with the name of Rāhula. In Ceylon's villages and in Colombo, the nation's capital city, among the illiterate and among the intelligentsia, Rāhula's name evokes respect and courage, with the exception that the self-seeking, oppressive, and corrupt among Ceylon's politicians fear and hate him.

Now that he concentrates his mental vigor on translating and interpreting Buddhism to Western scholars, he manifests the same fidelity to intellectual integrity that in other days characterized his efforts for the political emancipation of his native country. Western scholars find his friendship warm, lighthearted, and unconditional, but they sometimes experience discomfort from his uncompromising insistence on accuracy and clear thinking. In his own career he has exemplified the best of the heritage of the *bhikkhu.*

The Heritage of the Bhikkhu will fascinate the general reader. It will serve the scholar and teacher in the fields of history, social and political science, as well as those in the fields of Buddhist studies and comparative religions.

AUTHOR'S PREFACE

Since this book appeared in Sinhala in 1946 under the title *Bhikṣuvagē Urumaya,* several requests were made to me to publish it in English. But I could not find time to translate it. Dr. Edmund F. Perry, Professor and Chairman of the Department of History and Literature of Religions at Northwestern University, who came to know the book when he was Visiting Professor of Comparative Religion at Vidyodaya University in Ceylon, was interested in it and assigned its translation into English to Mr. K. P. G. Wijayasurendra as a part of his program as Visiting Scholar at Northwestern University (1969–1970). But for Dr. Perry's initiative, an English version of this book would perhaps never have seen the light of day. I am deeply grateful to him therefore, not only for this, but also for kindly taking upon himself the burden of writing a foreword at my request.

I thank Mr. Wijayasurendra for his faithful translation.

I am indebted to my venerable friends Māpalagama Vipulasāra Thera, Paṇḍita Piṁburē Sorata Thera, Attuḍāvē Guṇaratana Thera, Nāttaṇḍiyē Paññākara Thera and Dr. Hēnpiṭagedara Ñāṇāvāsa Thera, Professor of Buddhist Studies at Vidyodaya University, for providing me with valuable material for the postscript; and to Labuhēngoḍa Chandaratana Thera, Kaluvachchimullē Mahānāma Thera, both lecturers at Vidyodaya University, and to Kākkapalliyē Anuruddha Thera, lecturer at

Vidyālaṅkāra University, for some very useful discussions in London.

Finally, my gratitude is due to Professor E. F. C. Ludowyk for reading the manuscript and helping to improve this edition.

Walpola Rāhula
Northwestern University
Evanston, Illinois

INTRODUCTION TO THE SECOND SINHALA EDITION

The year 1946 marked the beginning of an important era in the history of modern Ceylon. A number of extremely significant and important events that left an indelible imprint on the history of Buddhism, the Sinhalese society, and politics occurred during this period.

In early January 1946, the Hon. D. S. Senanayake, the first Prime Minister of Ceylon, and some others voiced the opinion that Buddhist monks should not participate in public affairs. But knowledgeable and educated *bhikkhus* believed that Buddhist monks should continue their activity in public affairs as had been customary from the earliest times.

On January 26, 1946, at a public meeting held in Prince College, Kotahena, by way of an open public reply, I explained the fallacy of the view of Mr. Senanayake and his followers. The English- as well as the Sinhala-language newspapers carried a large number of letters and editorials for and against it. Some of the chief monks supported the position of the wealthy and the powerful and even went to the extent of issuing ecclesiastical injunctions through the media prohibiting the participation of *bhikkhus* in political activities.

The difference of opinion in the country was so great that the Vidyālaṅkāra Pirivena at Pāliyagoḍa deemed it necessary to make a declaration on the subject. Thus, on

February 13, 1946 the Vidyālaṅkāra declaration entitled "*Bhikkhus* and Politics" was issued. It stated that it was nothing but fitting for *bhikkhus* to identify themselves with activities conducive to the welfare of the people—whether these activities be labelled politics or not—as long as this activity did not impede the religious life of a *bhikkhu*. (See Appendix II.)

Four days later, at a public meeting of *bhikkhus* (*Saṅgha-sabhā*) held in the Bauddha Mandiraya (Buddhist Theosophical Society headquarters in Colombo) under the chairmanship of the Venerable Paṇḍita Palannoruvē Wimaladhamma Nāyaka Thera, it was resolved that *bhikkhus* alone should determine their course of action and that it was improper for laymen to interfere.

After this meeting, the situation became more serious and intense. Public enthusiasm and interest unseen in the country for well nigh a century was whipped up. The letters to the editor increased and more public meetings were held in the different districts of the country. *Bhikkhus* and laymen with progressive ideas and those with reactionary ideas split into two camps. The country was divided. There was hardly an issue on which so many letters and articles were written in the newspapers or so many public meetings held in this country. The powerful, reactionary conservatives, motivated by private considerations, made every effort to deny and destroy the freedom and rights that the *bhikkhus* had enjoyed from the earliest time.

On March 9, 1946, at a public meeting of *bhikkhus* and laymen, convened by the Buddhists of Kandy, with Dr. A. P. De Soyza as chairman, I gave a detailed academic exposition of the issue in a long speech. Many who listened that day repeatedly requested me to publish the speech as a pamphlet.

I found it extremely difficult to spare the time in those busy days. However, with the aid of the notes I had prepared for my speech, I began writing it as and when I could. Where necessary I also discussed some of the points with a few others. When completed I found it larger than I had anticipated. In that form the first edition was published in June 1946, under the title *Bhikṣuvagē Urumaya* (*The Heritage of the Bhikkhu*).

Public interest in this question was so keen that the first edition was sold out within three weeks of its publication. A second edition became very necessary. I was reluctant, however, to have a second edition without amending and revising certain sections and bringing the book up to date. Time still remained the determining factor and the appearance of the second edition had to wait.

The change brought about in Ceylon as a result of the upright course followed by the United *Bhikkhu* Council (*Eksat Bhikṣu Maṇḍalaya*)[1] in the recent past is tremendous. It was certainly responsible for the great awakening of the *bhikkhus* and laymen regarding current religious, social, economic, and political problems. *Bhikkhus* and laymen learned to speak the truth boldly, without fear, without servility to power and wealth. There was no other recent issue which evoked so much public enthusiasm.

The interest of this movement was not limited to Ceylon. Articles in newspapers and magazines of Asia and some of the European countries indicate the attention it received. The Hungarian weekly *Jövendö* said

[1] All notes appear in the back of the book.

the course of action adopted by the Buddhist monks in Ceylon should be taken as a lesson by the clergy in Europe.

As a result of this movement two important expressions with deep meaning and historical significance—"*Bhikkhu* Politics" and "Political *Bhikkhus*"—found their way into current Buddhist literature. "*Bhikkhu* Politics," as much as the *gantha-dhura* ("scholarship," literally "occupation of texts") may become a Buddhist tradition. Moreover, the "sons of the Buddha" (i.e., *bhikkhus*) who keep away from crooked and dishonest practices, who have a pure character, who have received a higher education in keeping with the needs of the times, who will not bow down before wealth or power, and will work for the benefit of the common man; altruistic, bold, upright, and honest monks will be regarded as political *bhikkhus*.

It is indeed gratifying to note that Mr. D. S. Senanayake and his followers, who primarily opposed the participation of *bhikkhus* in politics, seem to have of late realized their error and accepted our views and acted accordingly. The Ven. Nārada Thera of Vajirārāma in Bambalapiṭiya, Colombo, was sent to Singapore to settle some unrest due to bad conditions among the Ceylonese troops stationed there. It appeared that the Ven. Thera's mission failed to bring about the desired result. As the conditions worsened the soldiers mutinied. The Ven. Bhikkhu Kassapa (Dr. Cassius A. Pereira of lay name), with an army officer, was appointed as a committee by Mr. Senanayake and flown aboard a special plane to Singapore to inquire and report on the situation. This is the first time that a Buddhist monk was sent on such a mission since the reign of the ancient Sinhalese kings. It will be clear to anyone that these activities are not nonpolitical. It also appears that those chief monks (*nāyaka theras*) who were once opposed to *bhikkhus* taking part in politics now gave their blessings. We are happy to see that these worthy people are now awakening to the truth, though late.

In the course of preparing this second edition numerous changes have been made bringing the book up to date and a few chapters were added. In this respect the chronological chart and the appendices need special mention.

As I have mentioned earlier, many who read the first edition wrote to me offering constructive suggestions. While gratefully acknowledging these suggestions, I regret that available space is too limited and the list too long to mention each by name. However, I will be failing in my duty if no mention is made of the Ven. Telvattē Śrī Amaravaṃśa Mahā Thera and the Ven. Kōdāgoḍa Vijayasena Thera.

Several improvements in this edition were made on the suggestions of Mr. D. B. Dhanapala. I am deeply indebted to him for supplying me with certain facts. . . .

My thanks are due to the Ven. Hapugoḍa Siddhārtha and the Ven. Gallāllē Nandasāra Theras who read the proofs.

Finally I thank the Laṃkāputra Press for the interest shown in the printing of this book.

Walpola Rāhula
Vidyālaṅkāra Pirivena
April 1948

PREFACE TO THE FIRST SINHALA EDITION

This book was written hurriedly, in the midst of many other activities, when hardly any time could be spared for it. It is bound to contain many inaccuracies and I hope it will be possible to correct these in a future edition. I will be grateful for suggestions.

I am grateful to Professor Gunapala Malalasekera, my teacher at the University of Ceylon, with whom I had the opportunity to discuss profitably and meaningfully some of the points treated in this book.

I am also grateful to the Ven. Tripiṭakācārya Häḍipannala Prajñāloka Thera, a specialist in the *Vinaya,* who helped me with several problems of the *Vinaya* (disciplinary rules). It was the Ven. Prajñāloka Thera who made me aware of the clause in the Act of Appointment of chief monks (*nāyaka theras*) that those *bhikkhus* who received this high office from the Malvatta Chapter in Kandy should remain faithful to the British Government and spy on things said and done against that government.

I am deeply thankful to the Ven. Yakkaḍuvē Śrī Prajñārāma Thera, Director of the Vidyālaṅkāra Pirivena, the Ven. Tripiṭakācārya Koṭahēnē Prajñākīrti Thera, and Mr. D. B. Dhanapala, Principal of Dharmā loka College, Kalaniya, who not only offered information but also discussed many problems with me.

I remember with gratitude the encouragement given

me by the Ven. Paṇḍita Mādōviṭa Śrī Jñanānanda Thera, who showed much interest in this book in the several discussions I had with him.

Finally, my thanks and those of the readers are due in no small measure to my friend the Ven. Vinayācārya Nāttaṇḍiyē Paññākara Thera, who continually urged me to finish writing this book.

Thanks are also due Mr. Sirirsoma Ranasinghe, proprietor of Svastika Press, who spared no pains to print and publish this book in so short a period of time.

Walpola Rāhula
Vidyālaṅkāra Pirivena
June 1946

CHRONOLOGY

6th Century B.C.
- 563 Birth of Prince Siddhārtha Gautam
- 528 Enlightenment of the Buddha

5th Century B.C.
- 483 *Parinirvāṇa* of the Buddha
  - 1st Buddhist Council at Rājagaha

4th Century B.C.
- *circa* 383 Second Buddhist Council at Vesālī

3rd Century B.C.
- 269 Accession of Asoka
- 247 Third Buddhist Council at Pāṭaliputra
- 247–207 King Devānampiya Tissa
  - Mahinda Thera introduces Buddhism to Ceylon
  - The Sacred Bo Tree is brought to Ceylon
  - The Mahāvihāra at Anurādhapura is established
  - Writing of Sinhala Commentaries commences

2nd Century B.C.
- 199 Death of Mahinda Thera
- 198 Death of Saṅghamittā Therī

1st Century B.C.
- 101–77 King Duṭugämuṇu (Duṭṭhagāmaṇī)
  - Rise of religio-nationalism
  - *Bhikkhus* take an interest in social and political activities
  - Vesak festival held for the first time
  - Building of Lovāmahāpāya, Ruvanväli Dāgäba, Tissamahārāma, and Situlpavva

43–29 Bäminiṭiyā famine
Tipiṭaka committed to writing
Pariyatti (scholarship) takes precedence over *paṭipatti* (practice) and *paṭivedha* (realization)
The concept of *gantha-dhura* and *vipassanā-dhura*
Paṃsukūlikas and dhammakathikas

29–17 King Vaḷagambā (Vaṭṭagāmaṇī-Abhaya)
The establishment of the Abhayagiri Vihāra and its separation from the Mahāvihāra
Dhammaruci Nikāya (branch of the Vajjiputta Nikāya)

1st Century A.C.

38–67 Education is considered a special duty of *bhikkhus*

79–89 King Aḍagämuṇu proclaims the order of non-killing (*māghāta*) for the first time

89–92 King Kaṇirajānu-Tissa executes 60 *bhikkhus* who plotted against him

2nd Century A.C.

127–171 Buddha images (statues) and image-houses are mentioned for the first time (during the reign of King Vasbha)

3rd Century A.C.

248–249 Ekanāḷika famine

269–291 King Vohāratissa
Suppression of Vaitulyavāda
Purification of the *Sāsana*

4th Century A.C.

309–322 King Goṭhābhaya
Suppression of Vaitulyavāda and the banishment of Vaitulyavādins
Birth of the Sāgaliya sect in Dakkhiṇāgiri

334–409 King Mahāsena embraces Mahāyāna and destroys the Mahāvihāra
Dhammarucikas take residence in Mihintalē
Construction and donation of Jetavana to the Sāgaliya sect
The Mahāvihāra is deserted for the second time
Bodhisattva statues are mentioned for the first time
The Tooth relic is brought to Ceylon, during the reign of King Siri-Meghavaṇṇa (*circa* 371 A.C.)
The beginning of the Mahinda Festival (Poson Full Moon Festival)
Pāli *Suttas* are translated into Sinhala by Mahā Dhammakathī Thera
Fa-hien, the Chinese Buddhist monk, visits Ceylon

5th Century A.C.
Buddhaghosa Thera translates the Sinhala commentaries into Pāli
Mahānāma Thera writes the *Mahāvaṃsa*
Development of arts and crafts

6th Century A.C.
496–513 King Moggallāna I
The Hair relic is brought to Ceylon
The office of *asiggāhaka* is created
Purification of the *Sāsana*
524–537 King Silākāla
Jotipāla Mahāthera defeats the Vaitulyavādins
King of Kaliṅga, his queen, and minister arrive in Ceylon and receive Ordination
"Dharmadhātu" is brought to Ceylon from Kāsi

7th Century A.C.
611–617 King Moggallāna III
Recital of the *Tipiṭaka* and the purification of the *Sāsana*

Kaṭhina ceremony is mentioned for the first time

617–626 King Silāmeghavaṇṇa

Conflicts in Abhayagiri Vihāra

Purification of the *Sāsana*

New interest in the *Abhidhamma*

626–641 Rebels loot monasteries

650–658 Conflict between King Daṭhopatissa II and the Mahāvihāra

658–674 *Pirit* (*Paritta*) chanting is mentioned as a festival for the first time

676–711 Paṃsukūlikas attain a high position

8th Century A.C.

766–772 King Agbo VII purifies the *Sāsana*

Hindu practices infiltrate Buddhist practices

9th Century A.C.

831–851 King Sena I

Vājiriyavāda arrives in Ceylon

Pāṇḍya invasion of Ceylon

851–885 King Sena II invades Pāṇḍya

Purification of the *Sāsana*

Paṃsukūlikas separate from the Abhayagiri and form a different group

10th Century A.C.

The advancement and administration of Buddhist monasteries

12th Century A.C.

1153–1186 King Parākramabāhu the Great unifies the Three Sects

13th Century A.C.

1232–1236 Recital of the *Tipiṭaka* during the time of King Vijayabahu III and copying of Texts (manuscripts)

1236–1271 King Parākramabāhu II

Recital of the *Tipiṭaka* and purification of the *Sāsana*

1273–1310 Carrying away of the Tooth relic to Pāṇḍya and its recovery

14th Century A.C.

1356–1374 King Vikramabāhu III

Purification of the *Sāsana* under the leadership of Dhammakitti Maha Thera

1391–1397 Vīrabāhu II

Recital of the *Tipiṭaka* and purification of the *Sāsana* under the leadership of Dhammakitti II

15th Century A.C.

1473–1480 King Bhuvanekabāhu VI

Kalyāṇī Higher Ordination

16th Century A.C.

1505 The Portuguese arrive in Ceylon

1592–1604 King Vimaladharma I brings Higher Ordination from Rakkhaṅga

17th Century A.C.

1602 The Dutch arrive in Ceylon

1672 The French arrive in Ceylon

1684–1706 King Vimaladharmasūrya II brings Higher Ordination from Rakkhaṅga

18th Century A.C.

Välivița Piṇḍapātika Saraṇaṃkara Saṃgharāja Thera and his services

1750 King Kirti Śrī Rājasiṃha brings Higher Ordination from Siam

1796 The English capture the maritime provinces of Ceylon

19th Century A.C.

1815 The Sinhalese surrender to the English

The Kandyan Convention

1818–1848 Rebellions against the English

1847 Preparation of the Act of Appointment of *nāyaka theras* (high priests) with a view to make them loyal to the English government

1869 The first Buddhist school is founded in Doḍanduva

1873 Vidyodaya Piriveṇa at Māligakanda is founded

1875 Vidyālaṅkāra Pirivena at Pāliyagoḍa founded

1880 Buddhist Theosophical Society founded

1885 Ānanda College (Buddhist English Secondary School) founded

20th Century A.C.

National and religious revival

Buddhist societies and associations are begun

Bhikkhus receive modern education and come forward to serve the country

1938 The *Bhikkhu* Congress founded

1946 Vidyālaṅkāra declaration on *bhikkhus* and politics

1946 Laṅkā *Eksat Bhikṣu Maṇḍalaya* (United *Bhikkhu* Council of Ceylon) founded

1947 Political Declaration of Kälaṇiya

THE HERITAGE OF THE BHIKKHU

1. BUDDHISM AND SOCIAL SERVICE

Buddhism is based on service to others. Sumedha the Hermit (Bodhisattva who became Gotama the Buddha) renounced *nirvāṇa,* which was accessible to him, at the feet of the Buddha Dīpaṅkara and resolved to remain in *saṃsāra* (circle of existence and continuity) to serve the world. "He renounced *nirvāṇa* as suffering in *saṃsāra* and took upon himself suffering in *saṃsāra* for others as *nirvāṇa.*" A true Buddhist should have the strength to sacrifice his own *nirvāṇa* for the sake of others.

The Buddha exhorted his *bhikkhu* disciples not to settle permanently in one place, but to wander from village to village preaching to the people for their good and for their well-being.[1] Accordingly, the Buddha and his *bhikkhus* traveled throughout the year, except during the three or four rainy months (*vassāna*), preaching to the people ideas conducive to their well-being here and hereafter.

It is interesting to examine those ideas the wandering Indian *bhikkhus* preached. Generally, the villagers were poor, illiterate, not very clean, and not healthy. They needed simple moral ideas conducive to their material well-being and happiness rather than deep and sublime discourses on philosophy, metaphysics, or psychology as taught in the *Abhidhamma.* Ideas preached to such lay people are to be found in many places in the Buddhist Scriptures (*Tipiṭaka*).

The *Cakkavattisīhanāda-sutta* in the *Dīgha-nikāya* clearly states that poverty is a cause of crime and immorality. As the Buddha realized this fact, he and his disciples preached to the people the value of earning wealth and the importance of economic development for their well-being and happiness. Further in the *Kūṭadanta-sutta* (in the *Dīgha-nikāya*) he expounded that crimes such as stealing could not be stopped by punishment: for such crimes to be adequately and properly controlled and stopped, opportunities should be provided for the people to be happily engaged in their occupations and to lead comfortable lives.

A trader who desires to prosper in his business should exert himself constantly throughout the day; he should be able to select saleable goods; he should be able to determine the purchasing price and the selling price of a commodity; he should be capable of buying things where they are in abundance and selling them where they are in scarcity; he should not cheat his customers by using false measures and weights; he should not engage himself in "unjust trades."[2] Such interesting ideas about vocations are found in several places in the *Aṅguttara-nikāya*.[3]

Economic security (*atthi-sukha*), enjoyment of wealth (*bhoga-sukha*), freedom from debts (*anaṇa-sukha*), leading a faultless life (*anavajja-sukha*)—these are four kinds of happiness for a layman. Ability in one's occupation (*uṭṭhānasampadā*), protection of wealth (*ārakkhasampadā*), association with good friends (*kalyāṇamittatā*), expenditure in proportion to income (*samajīvikatā*)—these four are said to be conducive to the well-being of people in this world.[4]

People were advised to use a quarter of their earnings for day-to-day expenses, to invest two quarters, and to keep one quarter in reserve for emergencies. The ways in which accumulated wealth can be destroyed were also clearly explained.[5]

If a family that has become wealthy desires to live happily without falling from its position, it should regain things lost, should repair things which are damaged, should not be extravagant on food and drink, and should not have as the head of the family a man or a woman of ill-behavior and immoral life.[6]

It is stated in many places that for one's own advancement one should work strenuously without being lazy.[7] Health is the greatest asset and one should strive to be well.[8]

Numerous ideas for the well-being of society are frequently stated. Liberality (*dāna*), kindly speech (*peyyavajja*), service for the benefit of others (*atthacariyā*), equality (*samānattatā*)—these are well known as the four Bases of Assistance (*saṅgaha-vatthu*).[9] Many ideas for the advancement of society, as well as duties and obligations both by the family and the society for their mutual benefit, are mentioned in the discourses such as the *Sigāla, Parābhava,* and *Vasala*. The *Sigāla-sutta* goes even to the extent of stating that a husband should please his wife by making presents of beautiful dresses and ornaments to her.

During the time of the Buddha certain kings oppressed the people. It is evident from the *Dhammapadaṭṭhakathā* that the Buddha directed his attention even towards the serious problem of government through compassion (*karuṇā*), with a view to promoting a form of just government that would not harm and hurt the people suffering under the tyranny and the heavy taxes imposed on them by unrighteous rulers.[10]

Buddhism teaches that a country should be governed

in accordance with the Ten Duties of the King (*dasarājadhamma*), namely: (1) liberality (*dāna*), (2) morality (*sīla*), (3) giving up everything for the good of the people (*pariccāga*), (4) honesty and integrity (*ajjava*), (5) kindness and gentleness (*maddava*), (6) austerity in habits (*tapa*), (7) freedom from hatred, ill-will, enmity (*akkodha*), (8) non-violence (*avihiṃsā*), (9) patience, forbearance, tolerance, understanding (*khanti*), and (10) non-opposition, non-obstruction, *i.e.,* not to obstruct any measures conducive to the welfare of the people (*avirodha*).[11] When the Magadha monarchy prepared for war against the Licchavi Republic, representatives of the Magadha monarchy approached the Buddha and inquired of him if they would win that war against the Licchavis. The Buddha replied that the Licchavis would remain undefeated because seven conditions of welfare existed among them.[12]

Thus, in this way the Buddha and the *bhikkhus* taught such important ideas pertaining to health, sanitation, earning wealth, mutual relationships, well-being of society, and righteous government—all for the good of the people.

The Buddha did not confine his services to the mainland of India. He is reported to have visited Ceylon (Lanka) in order to settle a tribal feud.[13] Further, the *Samantapāsādikā* (*Vinaya* Commentary) states that the Buddhas of the past visited Ceylon for the benefit of the sick, in the interests of social welfare, and to settle disputes.[14] On one occasion when Ceylon was overwhelmed by an epidemic of fever, the Buddha Kakusandha visited this country with his *bhikkhus* and saved the people from death and disaster. On another occasion the Buddha Koṇāgamana visited Ceylon when it was in the grip of a severe and dreadful famine and saved the people from certain destruction. The Buddha Kassapa visited Ceylon on the occasion of a bitter strife, settled the feud, and brought peace and prosperity to the land and its inhabitants.

2. THE EVOLUTION OF THE LIFE OF THE *BHIKKHU*

Reading through the *Vinaya Piṭaka* we can clearly see that already during the life-time of the Buddha, the *bhikkhus'* way of life was beginning to undergo changes and modifications to suit the times and countries in keeping with their changing economic and social conditions.

At the beginning *bhikkhus* used robes made only of pieces of cloth discarded by the people at cemeteries and elsewhere. Later, on the request of Jīvaka, the Buddha approved the acceptance of other robes offered to them by devoted laymen. With this change in the earlier practice, people began to offer robes to *bhikkhus.* Sometimes devotees who went to the monastery with offerings of robes returned home taking them back as they could not find a *bhikkhu* to accept them. Thereafter the Buddha allowed the appointment of a Robe-Receiving *bhikkhu* for this purpose. However, those Robe-Receiving *bhikkhus* did not store them carefully and the robes were damaged and destroyed. Thereupon the Buddha approved the appointment of a Robe-Depositor *bhikkhu,* whose responsibility it was to store the robes. Nevertheless there was no appropriate place to store these robes and this resulted in the robes being destroyed by rats, white ants, and the like. Then the Buddha authorized the establishment of a store to keep the robes safely and also the appointment of a Store-keeper *bhikkhu* to be in charge. Differences of opinion arose among *bhikkhus* in distributing the robes collected in the store, whereupon the Buddha approved the appointment of a Robe-Distributor *bhikkhu* to distribute the collected robes among the members of the community. In this manner, more and more rules about robes were introduced.[1]

Even though it started with dusty, rag robes, the whole situation gradually changed with the acceptance of robes donated by devotees; one can see why new rules pertaining to robes had to be added from time to time.

How certain rules were changed or modified by the introduction of exceptions to suit occasions and circumstances is to be found in abundance in the *Vinaya*. For example, one may refer to the Disciplinary Rule on communal eating (*gaṇa-bhojana*) which was modified seven times to suit circumstances.[2]

Some *Vinaya* rules were changed to suit certain localities. According to the original rules of discipline, the presence of ten *bhikkhus* was essential for granting higher ordination (*upasampadā*) to a novice (*sāmaṇera*); footwear with more than one layer of leather should not be worn; bathing should be generally once a fortnight; leather should not be used as mats to sit on.

When these rules were in force, a *bhikkhu* named Soṇa from the Kingdom of Avanti, who was a pupil of the Elder Mahākaccāyana, spoke to the Buddha on behalf of his teacher: "Lord, it is very difficult to find *bhikkhus* in the country of Avanti. Therefore let the Blessed One approve that the number of *bhikkhus* required for granting Higher Ordination be reduced. The surface of the earth in the country of Avanti is very rough. May the Blessed One, therefore, permit the use of footwear consisting of more than one layer of leather? The people of Avanti appreciate frequent bathing. May the Blessed One therefore permit frequent bathing over there in that country? Just as the people of the Mid-Country use mats to sit on, the people of Avanti use hides to sit on. May the Blessed One therefore permit the use of hides as seats over there?"

Thereupon the Buddha summoned the *bhikkhus* to a congregation and changed the original rules, and declared that these new rules would be valid not only in Avanti but also in all other countries except the Mid-Country. Thenceforth the higher ordination ceremony could be performed by a gathering of any five *bhikkhus* with at least one of them learned in the *Vinaya;* the use of footwear with more than one layer of leather, frequent bathing, and the use of hides as seats came into practice.[3]

It is very clearly stated in the *Bhesajjakkhandhaka* of the *Mahavagga* that certain rules in regard to food and drink were relaxed and changed in times of famines for the convenience of *bhikkhus.*[4] At the beginning the Buddha had ruled that it was improper for a *bhikkhu* to keep foods inside his residence, to cook food inside his residence, and to cook his own food. He changed these rules when a famine ravaged Rājagaha. During this famine devotees brought *bhikkhus* such foods as rice, oil, salt, etc. Since it had been ruled as improper for *bhikkhus* to store these things inside their residences, they kept them outside where cats, rats, and other animals ate them and hungry people and thieves stole them. When the Buddha was made aware of this situation he approved the keeping of foods inside the residences. The *bhikkhus* did so. Yet the food was prepared outside their residences and hungry people came and watched. This caused a scandal and *bhikkhus* could not eat in peace. Thereupon the Buddha allowed cooking inside their residences. Much of the foods received during the famine was misappropriated by the attendants, leaving only a little for the use of the *bhikkhus.* The Buddha, being informed of this situation, permitted *bhikkhus* to prepare their own food. In the same way a few other rules on food were relaxed during this famine.

On a careful reading of the *Vinaya Piṭaka* one may clearly see that the Rules of Discipline were introduced and changed or modified in accordance with changing economic and social conditions to suit times and places.

The Buddha's system of controlling *bhikkhus* was purely democratic. Though he was indeed the undisputed master of the *bhikkhus,* he never desired to use that authority over them. A few months before his *parinirvāṇa,* the Buddha told the Elder Ānanda that he (the Buddha) never had the idea that he would lead the *Sangha* (the Order of Monks) or that the Order should depend on him.[5] Further, he admonished *bhikkhus* to take the *Dhamma* (truth, teaching) as their refuge, to make themselves their refuge, and to take no one else as their refuge.[6]

"Probably as a member of the clans which favored democratic constitutions, Buddha became imbibed with democratic ideas. He wanted to see his *Sangha* grow on democratic lines and framed the rules accordingly."[7]

The *Vinaya* (the Code of Disciplinary Rules for the *Sangha*) is not an absolute truth; it is only a convention agreed upon for the orderly and smooth life of a social organization. As it should be conducted according to social and economic changes to suit the place and the time, the Buddha laid down appropriate rules and also changed and modified them. Because he realized this, the Buddha, just before his *parinirvāṇa* (passing away), told Ānanda, his closest attendant disciple, that if the *Sangha* desired they could remove or abolish minor rules (precepts).[8]

3. THE COUNCILS

At the first Council held within a few months of the passing away of the Buddha this question about the minor rules (*khuddānukhuddaka-sikkhāpada*) was raised. Opinion among the *bhikkhus* was divided on the issue. The Council reproached the Elder Ānanda for not consulting the Buddha in order to clarify the question of minor rules.

In the distant past of 2,500 years ago things moved slowly. Even today in this atomic age, the economic and social structure of a country does not change drastically within two or three months. It is not possible that any important economic or social change in India could have taken place during the short period of a few months between the Buddha's *parinirvāṇa* and the first Council. Hence there was no necessity to change or abrogate even a minor rule. A *bhikkhu* by the name of Purāṇa, who heard about this Council, approved of it, but said that he would bear in mind the Doctrine (*Dhamma*) and the Discipline (*Vinaya*) as he had heard and learned them at the feet of the Buddha.[1]

A hundred years after the death of the Buddha the economic and social structure as well as the outlook of the people must have undergone changes. Differences of opinion in regard to the Rules of Discipline sprang up among the *bhikkhus*. The ten points raised by the Vajji *bhikkhus* of Vesali created controversy within the *Sangha*.[2]

Hermann Oldenberg, who edited the *Vinaya Piṭaka,* referring to this event, says:

> The ten points in question are extremely characteristic of the atmosphere in which the Buddhist community lived at the time. It was disputed whether the daily meal, in place of being partaken of at mid-day, might not also be partaken of when the shadows had attained the breadth of two fingers, and so forth.[3]

The second Council, held under the leadership of the Elders Yasa, Revata, and Sabbakami in the reign of King Kāḷāsoka, resolved that the ten points raised by the Vajji *bhikkhus* were against the *Vinaya.*[4] Those *bhikkhus* who disagreed with the resolution of this Council held a separate Council of their own, broke away from the sect of the *Theras* (Elders) and founded a sect named Mahāsaṅghika. Thus, in the next hundred years, due to differences of opinion over the Doctrine (*Dhamma*) and the Disciplinary Rules (*Vinaya*), eighteen sects arose, including those sects of the Elders.[5]

The late B. M. Barua, Professor of Pāli at Calcutta University, said:

> I cannot but agree with Dr. N. Dutt in thinking that the rise of the eighteen sects and schools of thought was rather a sign of health than that of distemper, rather a clear proof of the increased vitality and power of expansion and adaptability of Buddhism than that of its stagnation and death.[6]

Because of such differences and the division of sects, a third Council was held in the 3rd century B.C. during the reign of Emperor Asoka. After this Council the scope of activities of *bhikkhus* expanded further. With the royal patronage of Asoka a number of able and wise *bhikkhus* went to nine different countries as missionaries carrying with them the message of the Buddha and Buddhist culture.[7]

4. INTRODUCTION OF BUDDHISM TO CEYLON: THE NATIONAL RELIGION OF THE SINHALA PEOPLE

In the 3rd century B.C. during the time of King Devānampiya-Tissa (247–207 B.C.) Buddhism was introduced to Ceylon by the Arahant Mahinda, the son of Emperor Asoka. He brought not only the Buddhist religion but also the complete Buddhist culture, which had by then reached a very high standard of development. Ceylon was comparatively a less advanced country at the time. The Sinhala people progressed as a nation and won international recognition only after they embraced Buddhism. Sinhala literature, arts and crafts, architecture, town planning, education, health and sanitation, the ethics of the good life, economics, and politics—all these developed gradually under the guidance of Arahant Mahinda and the *bhikkhus*.

Mahinda's idea was to establish Buddhism firmly and permanently as the national religion and as the heritage of the Sinhala people and of their land. Unlike the Christian missionaries who came from the West in the recent past, Mahinda never thought of keeping to himself and his own country the ownership and authority over religion. It was because of this attitude that, in reply to a query from King Devānampiya-Tissa, Mahinda declared that Buddhism could not be deemed to have taken firm root in Ceylon until and unless a Ceylonese, born in Ceylon of Ceylonese parents, ordained in Ceylon, learned and recited the *Vinaya* in Ceylon.[1]

The matter of establishing Buddhism in a country in this manner is not found in the Pāli Canon. Nevertheless, Mahinda's desire was to make Buddhism the national religion of the Sinhala people. And it so happened.

Thenceforth the Sinhalese and Buddhism embraced each other inseparably. Buddhism became the state religion. From the time of the introduction of Buddhism in the 3rd century B.C. until the fall of the Sinhala Kingdom in the 19th century A.C.—during this long period of 2,200 years—it was the belief of the Sinhala people that the legal possession of the throne was the exclusive right of a Buddhist and none other.[2] This belief became so powerful by the 10th century that it is stated in an inscription of King Mahinda IV (956–972 A.C.) that not ordinary Buddhists but Bodhisattvas should become kings of Ceylon, and that that position had received assurance (*viyāraṇ*) from the Buddha.[3]

Further, the same inscription states that they, the kings, receive their office from the Great Community of Buddhist Monks (*Mahā Saṅgha*) in order to protect Buddhism.[4] Thus, it is quite clear that the approval of the *Sangha* was necessary for a man to become King of Ceylon. The *Mahāvaṃsa* states that in the 9th century the coronation ceremony was conducted in a monastery, in the presence of the *Sangha,* almost as a religious ceremony.[5]

The inscriptions of King Nissaṅkamalla (1187–1196 A.C.) state that Ceylon belongs to Buddhism and that non-Buddhist kings of such countries as Chola and Kerala have no right to the throne of Ceylon.[6]

This assertion is further explained and corroborated in the *Pūjāvaliya,* a book written in the 13th century:

> This island of Lankā belongs to the Buddha himself. It is like unto a treasury filled with the Triple Gem (Buddha, *Dhamma, Sangha*). Therefore the residence of false believers in this island will never be permanent as that of the demons (*yakkhas*) of bygone days was not permanent. Even though a non-Buddhist king may some time rule this land by force, his lineage will never be established in this country. This is a special power of the Buddha. Therefore, this island of Lankā is befitting only for the kings of right belief, and their lineal heritage will certainly be established and flourish.[7]

In a letter explaining the Sinhala law, sent by the Malvatta Chapter of the *Sangha* in Kandy to the Dutch governor of the maritime provinces of Ceylon (Governor Falk, 1765–1785), it is stated that the first rule that a king of Ceylon should observe is never to embrace any religion other than Buddhism.[8]

Historical evidence clearly shows that Buddhism existed as an institution of the Sinhala monarchy. To act against Buddhism was considered tantamount to treason. Therefore, the Sinhala leaders who supported the Tamil rule against the Sinhala king, immediately before the reign of King Dhātusena (460–478 A.C.), were indicted by Dhātusena on the charge that they did not protect either their king or Buddhism.[9]

The letter sent by the Malvatta Chapter to Governor Falk states that according to ancient Sinhala law, those who damaged or destroyed *dāgäbas* or sacred Bo trees were to be punished by death.[10]

There is ample evidence that even the Tamil kings

who invaded and ruled Ceylon from time to time governed as Buddhist kings. Perhaps they were never true Buddhists. Probably they pretended to be Buddhists for political convenience. The Tamil Khuddapārinda ruled Ceylon in the 5th century A.C. In an inscription, he prefixes the epithet "Buddha-dāsa" (servant of the Buddha) to his name, which certainly indicates his effort to appear as a Buddhist.[11] It is well known that the Tamil kings of the Kandy period embraced Buddhism and acted as Buddhists.[12]

The Sinhala government protected and guarded all such sacred objects like the branch of the Bo tree, the Bowl, Tooth, and Hair relics received from India, and religious edifices such as the Ruvanväli *dāgäba* as national treasures of the Sinhalese. After the arrival of the Hair relic of the Buddha from India, a special royal honorary title called *asiggāhaka* was created during the time of King Moggallān.[13] Even the popular festivals of the Sinhalese were mostly religious.

Thus, because of the unity of the religion, nation, and state, *bhikkhus* began to participate in many ways in public affairs and in the freedom and protection of the nation.

5. RELIGIO-NATIONALISM AND NATIONAL CULTURE

It was from the time of King Duṭugämuṇu (Duṭṭhagāmaṇī) that the religious and national fervor of both the laity and the *Sangha* began to grow intensely. In the middle of the 2nd century B.C. Anurādhapura was occupied by a Chola king named Eḷāra. The Sinhalese lost their freedom. The progress of Buddhism was arrested. The nation faced calamity.

The Sinhalese from the south (Ruhuṇa) mounted a crusade under the leadership of the greatest of national heroes, Prince Duṭugämuṇu, to liberate the nation and the religion from the foreign yoke. The young prince proclaimed to his fellow countrymen that he was not warring for the pleasures of kingship, but that it was for the re-establishment of Buddhism. Marching at the head of the advancing army, he carried a spear with a sacred relic of the Buddha enshrined in it. The Sinhalese were aware that the liberation of the religion was the liberation of their nation and rich and poor alike joined in this war.

In this decisive battle for the liberation of Buddhism and the Sinhalese, the *bhikkhus,* headed by their great Elders, did not remain confined to their cells. They joined the people and made their contribution to this great national enterprise. At this critical period, a dispute arose between Prince Duṭugämuṇu and his younger brother, Saddhā-Tissa. Realizing how detrimental it was to the national struggle, the Elder Godhagatta-

Tissa moved to unite the two brothers. A *bhikkhu* named Theraputtābhaya, at the time about to become an *arahant,* aroused and inspired by religious and national ardor, renounced the robes and joined the army. There is no doubt that many other *bhikkhus* like him renounced the Order of the *Sangha* to join the forces of liberation. At the request of Prince Duṭugämuṇu a large number of *bhikkhus* representing the Order of the *Sangha* accompanied the army. The Prince declared that the sight of *bhikkhus* was "auspicious" and "a protection." More and more people joined and supported the army when they saw the co-operation of the *bhikkhus.* Blessed and inspired by the presence of *bhikkhus,* the warriers fought with great courage and determination.[1]

From this time the patriotism and the religion of the Sinhalese became inseparably linked. The religio-patriotism at that time assumed such overpowering proportions that both *bhikkhus* and laymen considered that even killing people in order to liberate the religion and the country was not a heinous crime.

After the war, the victorious King Duṭugämuṇu (101–77 B.C.) one day became remorseful and penitent when he thought of the destruction of thousands of human beings in battle. Thereupon, eight *arahant bhikkhus,* as representatives of *arahants* living on the island of Piyaṅgu, came and spoke to the King as follows:

> By this deed there is no obstruction to thy way to Heaven. Only one and a half human beings have been slain here, O Lord of men. The one had taken the [three] refuges [taken the Buddha, *Dhamma,* and *Sangha* as refuges], the other had taken on himself the

five precepts [*pañca-sīla*]. Unbelievers and men of evil life were the rest, not more to be esteemed than beasts. But as for thee, thou wilt bring glory to the religion of the Buddha in many ways. Therefore cast away care from thy heart, O ruler of men.[2]

The *Mahāvaṃsa,* the Great Chronicle of Ceylon, states this to be an utterance made by eight *arahants.* Nevertheless, it is diametrically opposed to the teaching of the Buddha. It is difficult for us today either to affirm or to deny whether the *arahants* who lived in the 2nd century B.C. did ever make such a statement. But there is no doubt that Mahānāma Thera, the author of the *Mahāvaṃsa,* who lived in the 5th century A.C., recorded this in the *Mahāvaṃsa.* It shows that responsible *mahā theras,* as well as the ordinary *bhikkhus* and laymen, had accepted this idea, at least in the 5th century A.C., so that it is to be recorded in writing. Working for the freedom and uplift of the religion and the country was recognized as so important and noble that the Sinhalese in the 5th century A.C., both laity and *Sangha,* seemed to have believed that *arahants* themselves had accepted the idea that even the destruction of human beings for that purpose was not a very grave crime. What is evident from this is that the *bhikkhus* at that time considered it their sacred duty to engage themselves in the service of their country as much as in the service of their religion.

There are many examples illustrating how during the reign of King Duṭugämuṇu *bhikkhus* assumed a leading role in all national and cultural activities. There were *bhikkhus* who were expert even in such skills as architecture. The *Mahāvaṃsa* states that the plan of the nine-story Lohapāsāda was drawn by some *arahants* at the request of King Duṭugämuṇu.[3] The Relic Chamber of the Ruvanväli *dāgäba* was planned by Arahant Indagutta, and he supervised the construction of the whole edifice.[4] Moreover, the *bhikkhus* rendered even manual labor by supplying the masons with bricks and mortar.[5]

From the time of King Duṭugämuṇu the Sinhala *bhikkhus* began to take an increasingly keen interest in religious and national service. They also played a leading role in extremely responsible and highly political activities such as the selection and appointment of kings. After the death of King Saddhā-Tissa (77–59 B.C.) Prince Lajji-Tissa should have become the King of Ceylon. However, for some reason or other, on the approval of the assembly of *bhikkhus* gathered together in the Thūpārāma Vihāra, Prince Thullatthana was selected to become the king.[6] After the death of King Vijayabāhu I (1055–1114 A.C.) the dead king's sister, her three sons, the ministers, and the *bhikkhus* met and offered the kingdom to the Yuvarāja.[7] At the death of King Rajādhirājasiṃha (1780–1798 A.C.) the ministers and the chief *bhikkhus* (*Nāyaka Theras*) conferred and appointed Śrī Vikramarājasiṃha to the Sinhala throne.[8]

"Before innovations of importance are carried into effect, it is customary to consult the principal chiefs, and frequently the principal priests, and when other matters of public moment are in agitation the same persons are usually called into his [king's] council."[9]

Thus, from the earliest period of Ceylon history to the recent past, it is abundantly clear that in addition to participating in numerous other responsibilities, the *bhikkhus* played a leading role even in the highly responsible political function of selecting a suitable king to rule the country.

6. FUNDAMENTAL INNOVATIONS

The 1st century B.C. was a remarkable period, within which a considerable amount of changes took place both in Buddhist thought and in the way of the life of *bhikkhus*. A Brahamin named Tissa from Ruhuṇa in the southern part of Ceylon declared war against King Vaḷagambā (Vaṭṭgāmaṇī-Abhaya) who ascended the throne in the middle of that century. Meanwhile, the Tamils invaded Ceylon, drove King Vaḷagambā away, captured the capital city of Anurādhapura, and began to rule the country. At the same time a dreadful famine, well known in Ceylon history as the "Bämiṇiṭiyā sāya," the like of which was unknown and unheard of, devastatingly swept over the country. As a result of this calamitous situation the nation and the religion went from bad to worse.

King Vaḷagambā hid in a remote village with a few of his ministers. He was secretly raising an army to drive the enemy away from the land. However, one day under sudden provocation the king killed one of his ministers. The other ministers, deeply dissatisfied with their king's brutal behavior, deserted him, intending, perhaps, to join the enemy. These deserting ministers who were waylaid by bandits were rescued by a *thera* named Mahā-Tissa who was resident in Hambugallaka (Kemgalu) Vihāra. Thera Tissa, on learning the story of the ministers, was deeply moved realizing the great calamity that was to befall the nation and the religion as a result of this split between the king and his ministers, explained the dire situation and pleaded with the ministers to forget their grievances and to reconcile themselves with the king to meet the need of the hour—the liberation of Buddhism. The ministers agreed. Tissa Thera brought about a lasting unity between the king and his ministers.

Who could possibly say what the fate of the Sinhala nation and Buddhism would have been had this *thera* not intervened at this critical juncture? Today we are perhaps incapable of making a full evaluation of the religious and national service rendered by this Tissa Thera. Nevertheless, in his day King Vaḷagambā and his ministers realized that the country was indebted to him. Therefore, on behalf of the nation, as a mark of gratitude, King Vaḷagambā built the great Abhayagiri Vihāra and offered it to Tissa Thera. The ministers, too, built separate temples individually and offered them to Tissa.[1]

Ceylon had to face some terrifying misfortunes as a result of the Bäminiṭiyā famine during the time of King Vaḷagambā. Some people even turned into cannibals! *Bhikkhus* had no means of livelihood. While some fled to India, others took to the mountain regions in central Ceylon and led very miserable lives. Many people, both *bhikkhus* and laymen, died of starvation. Temples were deserted. The jungle invaded the premises of the Mahāvihāra and Ruvanväli *dāgäba* in Anurādhapura.[2]

On account of these disastrous conditions, several noteworthy fundamental changes and modifications with regard to Buddhism and the way of life of *bhikkhus* took place during this period.

The far-sighted *theras* (Elders) realized that it would be well nigh impossible to perpetuate the *Tipiṭaka*

(Buddhist Scriptures) by oral tradition (as was done till then) if they had to confront similar calamities in the future. Therefore, for the first time in history, these *theras* committed the *Tipiṭaka* to writing at Aluvihāra in Mātalē.

According to the original teaching of the Buddha, the practice of virtues (*paṭipatti*) and the realization of *nirvāṇa* (*paṭivedha*) are far more important than the mere study of the Doctrine (*pariyatti*). And this is well-known among all Buddhists. Nevertheless, differences of opinion regarding this idea arose among the *bhikkhus* who assembled after the Bämiṇiṭiyā famine mentioned earlier. What is the foundation of the Religion (*Sāsana*)? (The study of) the Doctrine or the practice of virtues? This question, unheard of before, was raised at this congregation. One is left to surmise that the chief reason for such a question was the effect on the minds of the people of the dreadful famine and other hardships.

In the debate that followed the *paṃsukūlika bhikkhus* (ascetic monks) said that the foundation of Buddhism was the "practice" (*paṭipatti*), while the *dhammakathika bhikkhus* (learned monks who were teachers and preachers) maintained that the foundation was the Doctrine (*pariyatti*). Both camps adduced facts and arguments for their views. Eventually it was resolved that the study of the Doctrine was more important than "practice," and therefore the study of the Doctrine constituted the foundation of the Religion (*Sāsana*). The *dhammakathika bhikkhus* won the day and the *paṃsukūlika bhikkhus* remained silent.[3]

So the Commentary to the *Aṅguttara-nikāya* says: "Even if there would be a hundred or a thousand *bhikkhus* engaged in 'insight-meditation' (*vipassanā*), if there would be no [study of the] Doctrine, then there could be no realization of the Noble Path."[4]

In conformity with this idea the Commentaries to the *Dīgha-nikāya* and the *Majjhima-nikāya* state: "The realization and the practice there may or may not be; [the study of] the Doctrine is sufficient for the stability of the *Sāsana* [Religion]. Indeed a wise man [*paṇḍita*] learns the *Tipiṭaka* and fulfills even the other two [practice and realization]. . . . When [the study of] the Doctrine [scholarship] is stable, the *Sāsana* is stable."[5]

Further, the Commentary to the *Vibhaṅga* states that it is a great error to belittle the importance of the study of the Doctrine.[6]

However, the opinion of the Commentaries cited above is different from the original idea found in the *Dhammapada,* which says that a person who practices the *Dhamma,* though his learning is little, is worthier than the one who learns much but does not practice it.[7]

Nevertheless, as time went on, due to social changes and the change of outlook of the people, "scholarship" had to be considered more important than "practice" and meditation. Scholarship rendered a great service to society, hence it was highly respected. The solitude-loving meditator lives in seclusion away from society, doing no service to society. The scholar is engaged in service which is necessary for society, and valued by it. It is therefore natural that a learned person who works for society should be highly esteemed. Because of this, "scholarship" came to be considered superior to practice and realization of the *Dhamma.* One cannot help believing that it was "scholarship," the power of intelligence and knowledge, that enabled the *dhammakathika bhikkhus* to establish their point of view defeating the *paṃsukūlika bhikkhus,* though the latter were in conformity with the fundamental teachings of Buddhism.

In this way, these two classes—the *paṃsukūlikas,* who dwelt in secluded places engaged in meditation, and the *dhammakathikas,* who lived in rural and urban areas with the people and worked for the well-being of society —appear to have continued as two classes right down to the present day. It is reasonable to believe that the forest dwellers (*araṇyavāsi*) and village dwellers (*grāma-vāsi*) referred to in later Covenants (*katikāvat*) are the same as these two classes. The forest dwelling *bhikkhus,* dissociating themselves from social activities, led a solitary life in the forest areas, devoted to meditation. The village-dwelling *bhikkhus* lived among the people, working for their well-being and uplift, engaging in social, educational, and cultural activities.[8]

Later on these forest-dwelling *bhikkhus* too, like the village-dwelling *bhikkhus,* took even to such literary pursuits as writing on secular subjects. This is proved by the *Bālāvabodhana,* a Sanskrit grammar written by the forest-dweller, the Ven. Dim̆bulāgala Mahā Kāsyapa. It is probable that by this time they were forest dwellers only in name, but for the most part they behaved like the village-dwelling *bhikkhus.* Undoubtedly these forest-dwelling *bhikkhus* also must have realized that the village-dwelling *bhikkhus'* way of life was more useful and beneficial and won the respect of most people.

7. STUDY AND MEDITATION: ACADEMIC DEVELOPMENTS

As described in the previous chapter, from the 1st century B.C. onwards there arose a greater interest in learning among the *bhikkhus,* an interest more pronounced than it had been before. As a result of this, two vocations were created: the vocation of study or scholarship called *gantha-dhura* (lit. responsibility or vocation of books or texts) and the vocation of meditation called *vipassanā-dhura.*[1] *Gantha-dhura,* or "scholarship," is the study and teaching of the *Dhamma* (Doctrine) while *vipassanā-dhura,* or "meditation," is insight-meditation or contemplation on life and existence as impermanent (*anicca*), as imperfect, suffering, anguish, unsatisfactory (*dukkha*), and as without any permanent, unchanging, eternal substance, self, ego, or soul (*anatta*). There is no mention of two such vocations in the original canonical texts of the *Tipiṭaka.*[2] This division is mentioned only in the Commentaries translated into Pāli in the 5th century A.C. and in subsequent literature. It may be inferred that the innovation of these two divisions was a result of the newly accepted theory that the "study of the Doctrine" constituted the foundation of the *Sāsana* (Religion).

From the illustrations given in the Commentaries it is evident that the vocation of study or scholarship (*gantha-dhura*) was deemed more important than the vocation of meditation (*vipassanā-dhura*). Able and intelligent *bhikkhus* who were strong in body and mind followed the vocation of scholarship, while *bhikkhus* of weaker intelligence, feeble in body and mind—particularly those who had entered the order in their old age—followed the vocation of meditation (*vipassanā-dhura*).

"I have become a monk in my old age. I am incapable of following the vocation of scholarship. Hence I will follow the vocation of meditation." This was said by the Elder Cakkhupāla.[3] The hunter Milakkha Tissa who lived in the Rohaṇa district became a *bhikkhu* in his old age. To his teacher he said: "Sir, [study of] the Text is the responsibility of the able. My faith has arisen as a result of suffering. I will follow the practice of meditation."[4] Having said thus, Milakkha Tissa Thera took his subject of meditation from his teacher, and practicing meditation, spent one day in Situlpavva, another day in Kataragama, and the next day in yet another place performing religious duties, wandering from place to place like a pilgrim.[5]

The above stories make it clear beyond doubt that scholarship was considered as belonging to the able, and meditation to the feeble, and that those who followed meditation did so because they lacked the capacity and ability necessary for scholarship.

Consequently, monks began to devote themselves primarily to studies and secondarily to meditation. Even in the study of the *Tipiṭaka,* the *Vinaya Piṭaka,* which teaches the practice of discipline, became less important than the *Abhidhamma Piṭaka* (philosophy and psychology) which develops knowledge. Thus the Mihintalē Slab Inscription of King Mahinda IV (10th century A.C.) states that the teachers who taught the *Vinaya Piṭaka* (Discipline) were paid 5 vasags, *Sutta Piṭaka* (discourses) 7 vasags, and *Abhidhamma Piṭaka* (philosophy and psychology) 12 vasags as allowances for their maintenance.[6] The salary paid to the teacher who taught the *Abhidhamma Piṭaka* was equal to the total salary paid to the two teachers of the other two *piṭakas*. Thus it is very clear that the *Vinaya Piṭaka* which taught "discipline" was placed third, while the *Abhidhamma Piṭaka*, conducive to the advancement of knowledge and which was subsequent to the *Vinaya* and *Sutta Piṭakas* in development, was placed first.

At first the vocation of scholarship (*gantha-dhura*) implied only the study and the teaching of the *Tipiṭaka*. Yet, as time passed, subjects such as languages, arts, sciences, history, law, etc. came to be included.[7] Therefore, *bhikkhus* specialized in all these branches of learning and began to teach them to the people. They wrote treatises on such subjects as prosody, poetics, and history. From the royal prince down to the son of the village peasant, all children learned at the feet of the *bhikkhu*. Monks knew what was to be taught to each of them. Every Buddhist temple, every monastery, was a free school. Because of this system of free instruction, education and culture developed in the island. Learned monks were honored and respected by the people. Historical records contain numerous references to the State providing learned and useful *bhikkhus* with special salaries, attendants, and other expenses for their maintenance and comfort.[8]

Moreover, it is proved by the Commentaries and other ancient records that the *bhikkhus* knew and practiced medicine from very early times in a manner befitting to and keeping with their way of life. The *Vinaya* (Discipline) had permitted *bhikkhus* to attend medically on their fellow monks, five kinds of their associates, their parents, some other close relatives and a few others very closely related. The Commentary to the *Vinaya Piṭaka* reveals that some monks had given medical advice, in keeping with their proper way of life, even to others besides those mentioned above, and had even accepted presents and honoraria for such services.

When the queen of King Vasabha (127–171 A.C.) fell ill, one of her maids went and consulted the Ven. Mahāpaduma Thera, a specialist in the *Vinaya* (Discipline). Without saying that he knew no medicine, Mahāpaduma explained to other fellow monks, in the hearing of the maid, a medical preparation suitable for the illness of the Queen. The maid returned to the palace and administered that medicine according to the prescription she overheard. On being cured, the Queen went to the temple, placed at the feet of the *thera* three robes and 300 pieces of money and begged him to use them for the purpose of offering flowers to the Buddha. The *thera* accepted them as "the share of the teacher" and used them for the purpose of offering flowers.[9]

The *Bhesajjamañjūsā,* written by the Ven. Pasmula Mahā Thera, the *Yogārṇava* and the *Prayogaratnāvaliya* written by the Principal of Mayūrapāda Piriveṇa prove that the ancient *bhikkhus* wrote on medicine and propagated medical science in the country. A Sinhala paraphrase to the *Bhesajjamañjūsā* was written by the Ven. Väliviṭa Piṇḍapātika Saraṇaṃkara Saṅgharāja Thera.

Bhikkhus' efforts to diffuse a knowledge of medicine in the country and the opportunity available for free consultations gratified the people and their devotion and attachment to *bhikkhus* increased.

How complete the education of a Buddhist monk was in those ancient days can be seen in a story in the *Samantapāsādikā,* the Commentary to the *Vinaya Piṭaka,* where it is stated that a position equal to the post of

Chief Justice of Ceylon was held by a *thera* during the time of King Bhātiya (38–67 A.C.).[10] King Bhātiya, who came to learn how the Ven. Ābhidhammika Godatta Thera of the Mahāvihāra at Anurādhapura, a specialist in the *Vinaya,* had settled a case of a *bhikkhu,* was so pleased that he empowered the *thera* to dispense justice not only in disputes among monks and nuns but also in disputes among lay people. The king decreed by the beating of the drum that the verdict of the Ven. Godatta should be accepted as final and conclusive and that whosoever did not abide by this verdict should be subject to royal punishment.[11]

This shows that the *Sangha* and the laity as well as the king had recognized the Ven. Godatta Thera's legal acumen, high intelligence, impartiality, understanding, and compassion. The *Mahāvamsa* records that King Bhātiya particularly honored learned *bhikkhus* dedicated to scholarship (*gantha-dhura*).[12]

8. MONASTERIES: THEIR ADMINISTRATION AND MAINTENANCE

On account of the enormous services rendered by Buddhist monks towards the stability and the progress of the country, the educational and moral enlightenment of the people, the prosperity and happiness of society, kings bestowed extensive tracts of land, including large and small villages, on monasteries and temples for their maintenance and upkeep. It is evident from the Mihintalē slab inscription of King Mahinda IV and the Sanskrit inscription in Jetavana that special departments were established for the administration of large monasteries.[1]

With increasing wealth and landed property the economy of the monasteries changed, and along with it the way of life of *bhikkhus* began to change further. Ideas that developed down the ages were incorporated into the Pāli Commentaries in the 5th century A.C. by the great commentator Buddhaghosa. Though different from those found in the original Pāli Canon, these new ideas having gained religious sanction were thenceforth definitely accepted as proper and correct. The following are a few of the important changes.

Except for his parents, those attending on his parents, his own personal attendant, and a candidate for the Order of Monks, it was considered improper for a *bhikkhu* to give others the food (alms) he had received before partaking of it himself (*anāmaṭṭha-piṇḍapāta*). However, the *Samantapāsādikā* (Commentary to the *Vinaya Piṭaka*) states that it (*anāmaṭṭha-piṇḍapāta*) may be given to waylaying bandits, rebels, and chiefs at moments of grave danger in order to escape. Likewise, it was improper for a monk to give away the wealth or property of the *Sangha* (community of *bhikkhus*) to laymen. The same text, however, states that even the wealth of the *Sangha* could be given to robbers and rebels, with a view to saving it, should they come to plunder or destroy it.[2]

This handing out of the wealth of the *Sangha* to marauders, robbers, chiefs, and bandits came to be thought suitable only after the monasteries became wealthy, and in order to safeguard their wealth. This is further illustrated by the following story in the *Samantapāsādikā*.[3]

One day a marauder named Abhaya went to Mihintalē monastery with a number of his accomplices, intent upon plunder. Dīghabhāṇaka Abhaya Thera, the chief incumbent of the monastery, having learned of it, immediately caused food to be prepared of such provisions as rice and *ghee* (butter) received by the *Sangha* and served it to the marauders. The robbers were pleased with the hospitality they received from the *thera,* and instead of plundering the monastery they promised to protect it. The other *bhikkhus* blamed him for giving away the food that was the property of the *Sangha,* misusing his position as the chief of the monastery. Thereupon Abhaya Thera assembled the *bhikkhus* and said: "Those robbers came to plunder the wealth of the *Sangha* and the treasures of the *cetiya* (*dāgäba*). I entertained them with food, intending to prevent them from plundering these. Let us find out how much wealth has been spent on feeding them and let us also find out how much wealth has been saved by reason of my entertaining them."

What was spent by the *thera* on the robbers was much less than the value of one carpet in the monastery. The assembly of monks, therefore, approved the entertainment of the robbers by Abhaya Thera and agreed that no charge be made against him. At the end of the story the commentator admonishes a wise monk to consider it a great benefit to entertain people in this manner. In addition, the Commentary to the *Dīgha-nikāya* mentions that kings and robbers (bandits) should be entertained.[4]

It became necessary to approve "the entertainment of robbers" in order to protect the monastic wealth as the monasteries became wealthy. During the time of the Buddha when monasteries had no wealth, a problem of this nature never arose among those *bhikkhus* who lived by begging their food day to day.

Another new convention, which did not exist at the time of the Buddha came to be approved after the monasteries began to receive lands and villages and the economic position of the *Sangha* began to change. This new convention is known as *lābha-sīmā,* "revenue boundary."

"Revenue boundary" had not been approved by the Buddha. Nor was it an injunction of those Elders of the Councils where the Doctrine was recited and settled. Nevertheless, when kings and ministers built monasteries they would erect an inscribed pillar (boundary stone) fixing a boundary of a *gāvuta* (a little less than two miles) or half-*yojana* (about 3½ miles) or a *yojana* (about 7 miles) around, declaring that they would give all the produce within these boundaries to the monastery. This is known as the "revenue boundary."[5] This indicates the manner of land donations to monasteries.

The Buddha had decreed that *bhikkhus* should not accept male or female slaves.[6] But when the lands owned by monasteries increased, and with it the number of *bhikkhus,* servants had necessarily to be employed. A passage in the *Samantapāsādikā* shows that the servants given to monasteries were in fact slaves and that they could not be admitted into the Order of the *Sangha* without first being set free from slavery.[7] Because it was against the teaching of the Buddha for *bhikkhus* to accept slaves, the Commentary on the *Majjhima-nikāya* says that they (servants) should be accepted *not as* slaves but as attendants of the monastery.[8]

This, however, was only an expedient. That these people were *de facto* slaves, whatever the designation under which they were employed in the monastery, is quite clear from the above statement in the *Samantapāsādikā* which says that they should not be admitted into the Order of the *Sangha* without manumission.

The many ancient inscriptions and the *Mahāvaṃsa* prove beyond doubt that from very early times, from about the 2nd century A.C., slaves were employed in monasteries for various activities and to attend on *bhikkhus.*[9] Further, the inscriptions bear evidence to the fact that the monasteries employed not only male but also female servants.[10] That women were employed in the monastic establishments at Mihintalē is evidenced by such words as *jeṭmava* and *salājeṭak* (signifying female servants) in the Mihintalē inscription.

Similarly, even during the Kandy period, women acted as attendants upon monks. James Cordiner in his *Description of Ceylon* says: "All their [priests'] wants are supplied by the people and the most beautiful females in the country attend them in their houses without wages. So great is the sanctity of their character that a virgin who has served in their abodes is considered by the young men as an enviable wife."[11]

History as well as the inscriptions make it clear that kings had granted land to the monasteries for the maintenance of these male and female slaves or servants, while other wealthy people had deposited large sums of money for the same purpose.[12]

By the 10th century A.C., the wealth and the temporalities of monasteries had further increased. The administration of principal monasteries was carried on by State departments established for the purpose. Officials were appointed in charge of different functions, as well as minor servants to attend to even very small duties. All workers were paid fixed wages, which were paid even to the monks who looked after the monastery.

Bhikkhus who taught the *Tipiṭaka,* as well as those *bhikkhus* engaged in various other duties, were paid salaries in keeping with the nature of their work. Even the annual budget of the monastery was read before the monks for their approval.[13]

Sir John D'Oyly says that during the time of the Kandyan Kingdom all the chief monks (*nāyaka theras*) were included in State budgets and were paid salaries by the government. Each of these monks received up to a maximum of 150 silver coins, according to his rank or status and the position of his family.[14] In keeping with this ancient custom, up to this day, those *bhikkhus* who hold office in the Asgiriya and Malvatta monasteries in Kandy receive an allowance called *viyadam paḍiya* from the income derived from the lands granted by the ancient kings.

It is well known that during the time of the Buddha

monasteries did not possess land, wealth, slaves, or servants. *Bhikkhus* received no fixed salaries for their upkeep. There were no budgets to be approved by the congregation of *bhikkhus.* But with changing environmental circumstances and economic conditions, changing ideologies among the laymen as well as the monks, a new monastic way of life developed in Ceylon. It was not, however, the outcome of any special desire or instigation by any particular person or group. It was the natural result of the inevitable changing political, economic, and social conditions of the country from time to time.

Let us for a moment ask why *bhikkhus* were provided with a comfortable living, were granted such large tracts of land, provided with servants, and even State departments established for the management of their monasteries—all these done at the expense of the State, spending the national wealth. To believe that all this was done solely with a view to secure a happy life in the next world, a good future re-birth, is certainly an incorrect view of the dynamics of human society. A more reasonable and plausible explanation is that *bhikkhus* contributed in very great measure to the development and progress of the religion and the nation. They worked for the common welfare of the people and the cultural advancement of their country. It should surprise no one, therefore, that the state looked after the needs of the *Sangha.*

9. ARTS, CRAFTS, AND LITERATURE

Ananda K. Coomaraswamy, who was the curator of the Oriental Section in the Boston Museum and a scholar of international repute, says:

> Buddhism became indeed the chief patron rather than the opponent of fine arts, which spread with it from India to Ceylon, Burma, Siam, and Java in the south, and to China and Japan in the north. It thus came to pass that it was important for even the priests to have some knowledge of the theoretical side of craftsmanship at least, and this was often the case; they were rather expected to explain such works as *Sāriputta* to the less learned craftsman than to learn from him.[1]

The Books of the Discipline (*Vinaya*) reveal that from the time of the Buddha *bhikkhus* painted and encouraged others to paint. The *Cullavagga* and its Commentary state that it is not proper for a *bhikkhu* to paint figures of men, women, and animals or cause others to paint them. It does not befit a *bhikkhu* to ask a man to make the figure of even a door-keeper (guard).[2] Nevertheless, it is fitting and becoming for a *bhikkhu* to encourage others to paint such subjects as Birth Stories (*jātakas*) of the Buddha which promote delight and devotion in the people. A *bhikkhu* himself may paint or ask another to paint the flower and creeper motifs.[3]

Accordingly, Buddhist monks were eager either to paint or to have the shrine rooms of temples painted with Birth Stories and other events connected with the life of the Buddha which were exemplary and inspiring. They also built images or had them built. Further, it is a general tendency of the people to be attracted more to those temples decorated with beautiful carvings, paintings, and images. The *bhikkhus* therefore took a particular interest in building beautiful and artistic *vihāras* and *dāgäbas*. Thus the arts and crafts were encouraged and developed in Buddhist countries.

From the 5th century A.C. onwards the contribution made by *bhikkhus* towards the progress of culture, literature, arts, and crafts assumed even greater dimensions. By about the 4th and 5th centuries it seemed that no sculptor could compete with the Sinhala Buddhist monk in the art of making the Buddha statue. About the year 456 A.C. a *bhikkhu* by the name of Nanda with four other monks visited China as a cultural ambassador of Ceylon. Nanda Thera, who was a celebrated sculptor, presented the Chinese Emperor with a Buddha statue which he sculpted, an extremely exquisite and wonderful piece of craftsmanship. From a distance of about ten paces the statue appeared truly brilliant, but as one came closer to the image the features gradually disappeared. Kings and dignitaries of Central Asia sent able sculptors to procure copies of this statue, but none could execute anything similar to the Buddha image of Nanda.[4]

It is well known that even during the Kandyan period, the last and decadent period of the Sinhala kingdom, *bhikkhus* painted *vihāras*. The *jātaka* stories and other paintings in Degaldoruva and Ridī Vihāra were done by the famous artist-monk of the time, Devaragampala Silvatanne Unnanse, who lived in the 2nd half of the 18th century. These paintings, highly esteemed and appreciated by art critics, were executed under the supervision of the Ven. Moratoṭa Mahā Nāyaka Thera of the Malvatta monastery in Kandy.[5]

It should also be mentioned here that the Ven. Ratmalānē Śrī Dharmāloka Mahā Thera (1828–1887 A.C.), the founder of the Vidyālaṅkāra Pirivena at Pāliyagoḍa, when he was residing in the region of Satkōralē, renovated several dilapidated *vihāras* and himself executed the paintings there.[6]

The arts and literature began their development from the 5th century A.C. At the beginning of this century the Ven. Buddhaghosa Thera translated the Sinhala Commentaries into Pāli.

What should merit special mention about the 5th century in relation to the change and development of *bhikkhu* life is the writing of the *Mahāvaṃsa,* the history of the Sinhalese, by the Ven. Mahānāma Thera.

According to many *Suttas* in the *Tipiṭaka,* the Buddha had stated that it was improper for and unworthy of a *bhikkhu* to be engaged in commonplace talk about such subjects as kings, ministers, bandits, wars, cities, and provinces. But from cover to cover the *Mahāvaṃsa* contains stories about kings, ministers, bandits, wars and rebellions, towns, cities, and countries. Mahānāma Thera was more than aware of this injunction. However, the time required a systematically written history of the Sinhala nation and he decided to write it. Undoubtedly it was contrary to the teachings found in the *Suttas.* However, he discovered a device to exonorate himself from the blame for breaking the rule.

The Commentaries maintain that, at the end of a discussion about kings and ministers and others, if one reflects that "even such powerful personages were sub-

The Ruvanväli-säya at Anurādhapura (after restoration), the most venerated *dāgäba* (*stūpa*) in Ceylon, built in the 1st century B.C. by King Duṭugämuṇu (Duṭṭhagāmaṇī).

An assembly of *bhikkhus* convened by the Ẹksat Bhikṣu Peramuṇa on June 29, 1946 at Colombo Town Hall to discuss their role in national affairs. (Courtesy the *Times of Ceylon*)

A *bhikkhu* (the author) addressing a mass meeting on the Galle Face Green in Colombo. (Courtesy the *Times of Ceylon*)

The Ven. Māpalagama Vipulasāra Thera, Incumbent of the temple (standing left), the author (seated center), and their colleagues examine palm leaf manuscripts of the Pāli *Tipiṭaka* in the library of the Parama Dhamma Chetiya Pirivena at Ratmalāna. (Courtesy *Photo Pfältzer,* Hart/Chiemsee, Germany)

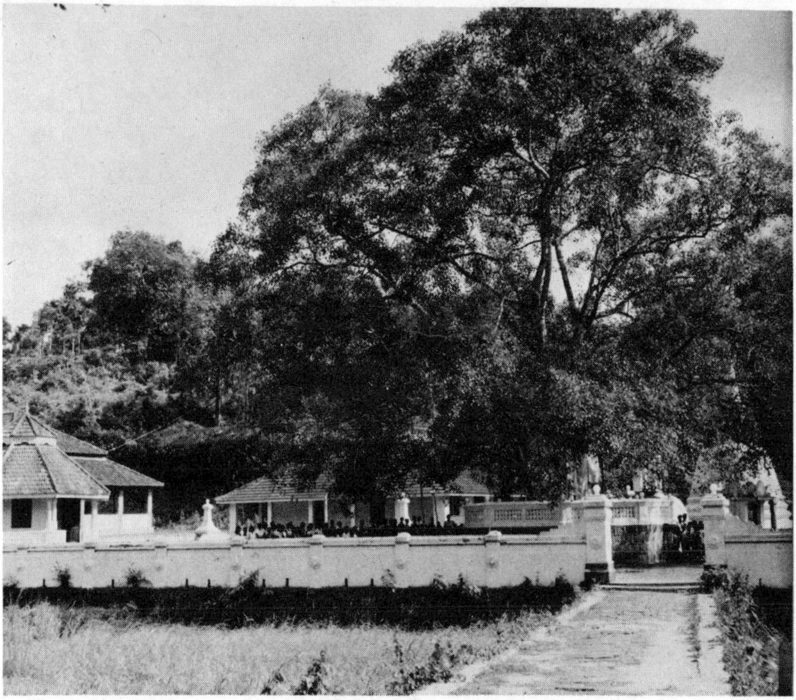

A class of children learning Buddhism under the historic Bo tree at Rāja Mahā Vihāra, Paragoḍa, the author's monastery. The *dāgäba* (*stūpa*) is beside the Bo tree.

Vidyodaya University (the main entrance showing a portion of the library and administration building).

On the campus of Vidyālaṅkāra University, the Ven. Nāttaṇḍiyē Paññākara Thera is seen in front of the library.

Minister of State and Mrs. J. R. Jayawardena are seated behind the *bhikkhus* at the Independence Day Celebrations in Kandy in 1969. In the front row is the author talking with the *mahā nāyaka thera* of the Rāmañña sect. (Courtesy *Photo Pfältzer,* Hart/Chiemsee, Germany)

At the Buddhist-Christian memorial service for the late Rev. Dr. Martin Luther King organized by the author (who at that time was Vice-Chancellor of the Vidyodaya University of Ceylon) and the Rev. Dr. Edmund F. Perry (at the time Visiting Professor of Comparative Study of Religions at Vidyodaya University), held at Vijayārāma Buddhist Temple, Gangoḍavila, near the University.

From left to right, the Ven. Dāmpe Ratanasāra Nāyaka Thera, Incumbent of the temple, the author and Dr. Perry are seen leading the University and community congregation in the ceremony of "transferring merits" to Dr. King.

ject to decay and death," that talk or discussion itself becomes a topic of meditation (*kammaṭṭhāna*).[7] So Mahānāma Thera terminated every chapter of the *Mahāvaṃsa* with a *gāthā* (verse) containing the idea of the impermanence of life or some other spiritual and religious admonition. And further, each chapter ends with a formula which says that "the *Mahāvaṃsa* was written for the serene joy and emotion of the pious." This is how the learned *thera* avoided the blame of writing history books containing talk of "commonplace" things.

The author of the *Dīpavaṃsa,* too, after enumerating the names from King Mahāsammata down to Prince Siddhattha (the Buddha's first name), suddenly inserts the verse beginning with *aniccā vata saṃkhārā,*[8] signifying the impermanence of all conditioned things, as if he had recited the whole list of names of the Mahāsammata dynasty in order to prove the impermanence of things! This, too, was in conformity with the idea expressed in the Commentaries.

Wilhelm Geiger, who edited and translated the *Mahāvaṃsa,* says that there is hardly a corner of the Indian continent whose history is chronicled as well as Ceylon's.[9] Had Mahānāma Thera not written the *Mahāvaṃsa,* the Sinhala people would have been deprived of the proud privilege of possessing an unbroken and complete history.[10]

The writing of the *Mahāvaṃsa* was a definite sign of the greater participation of *bhikkhus* in national activities. From this time onwards they began to engage in public affairs.

It is not proposed to describe here the great contributions made by Buddhist monks to the development of Sinhala civilization, culture, and literature during the

Poḷonnaruva, Daṁbadeṇiya and Kōṭṭe periods since these are already well known to students of Ceylonese history. Suffice it to say that if we have any literature of which we can be proud of, virtually all of it was written by *bhikkhus*. A contemporary Sinhala novelist went so far as to praise the *bhikkhus* for having saved Sinhala civilization and culture from the sex maniacs![11]

10. NATIONAL FREEDOM AND THE PROTECTION OF PEACE

In the middle of the 5th century Ceylon was again invaded and ruled by the Hindu Tamils from South India. There were no Sinhalese strong enough to save the country from the aggressor. At that time a certain learned, virtuous, and farsighted monk discovered and raised a royal prince named Dhātusena, his nephew, both wise and valorous, and fit to be the King of Ceylon. (Some think that this Elder was none other than Mahānāma, the author of the *Mahāvaṃsa.*) The *thera* admitted this prince into the Order and brought him up secretly, giving him an education suitable for a ruler. The Tamils made several attempts to kill the prince. The Elder took his young novice in disguise from place to place and protected him until he came of age. Dhātusena learned diplomacy and the laws of government necessary for a king at the feet of his uncle, the *thera.*[1] This is a clear indication of the high degree of learning among the *bhikkhus* at the time. When Dhātusena came of age, he left the Order, collected an army, defeated the Tamils and once again liberated the Sinhalese and Buddhism from foreign rule.[2]

None can say for how long the Sinhalese and Buddhism would have suffered this foreign domination if this *mahā thera,* devoted to his religion and to the freedom of his nation, had not raised Dhātusena and inspired him to liberate his country.

King Kassapa (478–496 A.C.) killed his father, King Dhātusena (460–478 A.C.), and ascended the throne. Kassapa, the builder of the famous rock fortress Sīgiriya, suffered the displeasure of the *Sangha* because he was a patricide. For the same reason he was disliked by his subjects. The *bhikkhus* spared no effort to depose the unrighteous Kassapa and enthrone his brother, the righteous Prince Moggallāna in his place. The *Mahāvaṃsa* states that Prince Moggallāna assembled his army in a monastery named Kuṭhāri.[3] The monks recognized it to be their duty to the nation and to Buddhism to depose an evil-doer, who ruled by terror, and, together with Prince Moggallāna, they succeeded in dethroning King Kassapa.

The monks of the Mahāvihāra, having swept clean the temple premises, donned their robes and lined up in array to welcome King Moggallāna I (496–513 A.C.) who had ridden to victory with their support.[4] The grateful king, recognizing their assistance, paid the first call of his reign to the monastery. As if it were to indicate that the symbol of royalty, the white parasol, belonged more to the *Sangha* than to himself, he offered it to the *bhikkhus* who, in turn, returned it to the king.

The history of Ceylon bears repeated evidence to the fact that whenever the occasion arose for monks to contribute their share, in whatever form or manner, for the protection of the country and the religion, they have unflinchingly risen to the needs of the hour. Likewise, it was customary for these kings of the past to consult the *bhikkhus* on all important occasions and problems.

King Mahinda II (772–792 A.C.), when he prepared to declare war against the Rohaṇa district, summoned a meeting of the *Sangha* and the wise, elderly people at

Thūpārāma temple and obtained their approval.[5] This was done because the approval of the *Sangha* was a sure and certain way of enlisting the cooperation of the people, for the *bhikkhus* then had much influence.

A bitter political feud between the Viceroy Mahinda and King Sena II (851–885 A.C.) was settled by the intervention of the *Sangha,* which brought about a peace treaty between the two contending parties.[6]

A political rift between the Ādipada Mahinda and King Kassapa IV (896–913 A.C.) plunged the country into a civil war. Once again, the *bhikkhus* intervened to bring about an amicable settlement and restored peace and stability in the land.[7]

Hundreds of human lives were unnecessarily destroyed by a bitter political quarrel that erupted during the time of King Udaya III (945–953 A.C.). A major civil war was in the offing. *Bhikkhus* again saved the country and the religion from an impending catastrophe.[8]

King Vijayabāhu I (1055–1114 A.C.) appointed his brother, Prince Jayabāhu, as viceroy with the full assent of the *bhikkhus.*[9] The council which assembled to select Prince Jayabāhu as king, upon the death of King Vijayabāhu, included some leading *theras.* The dead king's sister, her three sons, and the chief ministers were present. The *bhikkhus* voted with those assembled and Prince Jayabāhu was unanimously (*samānacchandataṃ gatā*) appointed king.[10]

Once more the *bhikkhus* settled the perilous political strife between Mānābharaṇa and King Gajabāhu II (1137–1153 A.C.), and the civil war between King Gajabāhu II and King Parākramabāhu I (1153–1186 A.C.) and restored peace in the country. In the latter incident they even had a peace treaty (*sandhāna*) signed between the contending princes.[11] Two inscriptions in Maṇḍalagiri Vihāra and Saṃgamu Vihāra record the peace treaty made between Parākramabāhu and Gajabāhu. Dr. S. Paraṇavitāna surmises that these two *vihāras* were probably the residences of the principal monks who, on either side, exerted themselves to bring about a reconciliation between the rival rulers. He conjectures further that perhaps the documents were engraved on stone at the insistence of the monks who considered this necessary to ensure the faithful observance, by both parties, of the agreement.

The *Pūjāvaliya* says that when King Parākramabāhu the Great, with a large army collected from all over Ceylon, was ready to leave for India on a crusade to spread the "Right Faith" after conquering that country, the *Sangha* did not allow him to go abroad. So the king stayed behind and sent only his army.[12]

King Kalikāla Sāhityasarvajña Paṇḍita Parākramabāhu (1236–1271 A.C.)[13] consulted the *bhikkhus* and obtained their advice in order to decide who was likely to be his best successor among six princes. In accordance with the approval of the monks, Vijayabāhu IV, also known as Bōsat Vijayabāhu (1271–1273 A.C.), was appointed king.[14]

In the beginning of the 15th century there was much confusion and chaos regarding the throne of Ceylon. For two or three years there was almost an interregnum as a result of the contending factions. At that time an elder (*thera*), the chief of the Vīdāgama Vihāra, adopted and educated a young son of Queen Sunetrā, and when he was sixteen years of age, entrusted him to the army and had him crowned as Śrī Parākramabāhu (also known as Parākramabāhu VI, 1412–1467 A.C.).[15]

In 1760 A.C., Governor Falk, the Dutch administrator

of the maritime provinces, sent a series of questions seeking clarification on the Sinhala constitution, laws, habits, and customs, to the Sinhala government in the Hill Country (Kandy). These queries were answered not by Sinhala ministers, but by the Council of the *Sangha* (*Sangha-sabhā*) of the Malvatta Chapter, headed by the Ven. Väliviṭa Piṇḍapātika Saraṇaṃkara Sangha Rāja Thera.[16]

Moratoṭa Rājaguru Dhammakkhandha Mahānāyaka Thera and another monk from the District of Galle acted as delegates to negotiate a trade pact between the Sinhala Kingdom in the Kandyan Provinces and the English in the maritime provinces of Ceylon. Moratoṭa Mahānāyaka Thera appeared as the king's ambassador on this mission.[17]

Whatever had to be done for the protection, peace, and development of the country—political or otherwise—was recognized by the *bhikkhus* of the past as their task to be accomplished readily and prudently.

11. THE PORTUGUESE PERIOD

The Portuguese first arrived in Ceylon in 1505 A.C., during the reign of Vīraparākramabāhu VIII. As a result of internecine feuds the country by this time was in disintegration. It had broken up politically. In several provinces local chieftains posed as kings. The Jaffna peninsula was controlled by the Tamils. The Vanni provinces were ruled by chieftains known as Vanniyars. Petty rulers continued to govern small towns such as Badulla, Gampola, Pērādeniya, Mādampe, Ambulugala, Uḍugampola, and Devundara. Although the King of Kōtte (capital of Ceylon at the time) was deemed the principal monarch of Ceylon, there was no direct communication or cooperation between him and the provincial rulers. They acted independently and ruled their domains as they pleased. They were constantly at war with each other. They had neither the strength nor the opportunity to do anything to help the development of the country. Economically, Ceylon was in decline. The seaports along the coast with their flourishing trade were dominated by the Moslems. Education and culture were at their nadir. With the general degeneration of the island the position of Buddhism and *bhikkhus* declined.

This weakness gave ample opportunities for the Portuguese to establish and stabilize their rule over the maritime provinces without much effort. Warfare with the invading Portuguese further enfeebled the Sinhala government. The Portuguese deprived the Sinhalese of both their freedom and wealth and decimated them. Nothing worthy of mention was done for the development of the provinces they ruled. However, special care was taken to propagate Roman Catholicism. To achieve this the Portuguese resorted even to killing, torturing, and brutalizing the native population. A non-Christian was considered an enemy of Portugal and Jesus Christ. The power of the Roman Catholic missionaries who accompanied the Portuguese began spreading in the maritime districts of Colombo, Pānadura, Maggona, Bēruvala, Galle, and Wäligama. Roman Catholicism spread also in the Jaffna peninsula. In order to procure employment under the Portuguese government many Sinhalese embraced the Roman Catholic religion. Association with the Portuguese turned the Sinhalese into liquor addicts. Even though some of the Sinhalese appeared to be Roman Catholics in public, solely for materialistic gain, secretly and in private they professed Buddhism as their true religion. Occasionally even some Sinhalese kings, princes, and princesses accepted the Roman Catholic religion out of political considerations.

During the reign of the patricide Rājasiṃha I (1581–1592 A.C.), who gave up Buddhism and embraced Hinduism, Buddhism and the *bhikkhus* suffered severely as a result of his atrocities and his fierce wars against the Portuguese. Rājasiṃha I killed many *bhikkhus* and burned a large number of religious and literary books. The brutality and cruelty of this king were so terrifying that the people of the Kandyan Provinces were even willing to help the Portuguese against him. The Portuguese, grasping it as a golden opportunity to bring the whole country under their sway, led an army to Kandy, accompanied by two Sinhala princes who had embraced Roman Catholicism and attempted to capture the

Kandyan Provinces. This attempt failed. The Portuguese, however, ruled the maritime provinces of Ceylon for a period of 153 years, from 1505 to 1658.

Internal quarrels and ceaseless warfare between the Sinhalese and the Portuguese for several generations made it absolutely impossible for anything to be done for the country and the emancipation of its people. The national culture and religion degenerated and deteriorated. Because of the brutal and cruel behavior of Rājasiṃha I some monks abandoned their robes to lead a lay life. It was indeed a sorry state of affairs for the *bhikkhus,* so much so that it was difficult to find a fully ordained *bhikkhu* in the country. Therefore, King Vimaladharma I (1592–1604 A.C.) sent a deputation of ministers to the Rakkhanga Country (modern Arakan in lower Burma) and obtained *bhikkhus* with higher ordination and caused the *upasampadā* or higher ordination ceremony to be performed on a dais built on the Mahaväli River at Gäṭaṁbe Ford (*udakukkhepa-sīmā*).

12. THE DUTCH PERIOD

The Dutch appeared in Ceylon in 1602 A.C. The Sinhala kings attempted to drive the Portuguese out with the assistance of these new arrivals, and this resulted in more warfare. Together, the Sinhalese and the Dutch fought the Portuguese for just over a half century, until Portuguese power in Ceylon was completely destroyed in 1658 during the reign of King Rājasiṃha II (1634–1684 A.C.). The maritime provinces fell into the hands of the Dutch.

At the beginning the Dutch were friendly towards the Sinhalese. They had promised to return all of the maritime fortresses to the Sinhala king once the Portuguese were defeated. But when the Portuguese were driven away the Dutch forgot their promise. They retained the fortresses and began to govern the maritime provinces. The Sinhalese were, therefore, compelled to wage war against the Dutch.

In 1672 a French fleet arrived in Ceylon. King Rājasiṃha II, who learned that the French were against the Dutch, permitted them to build a fortress near the harbor of Trincomalee, with the hope of getting their help to defeat the Dutch. The king's intention and expectations failed. The Dutch captured the French garrison in Trincomalee and the hope of the French to establish a permanent settlement in Ceylon and rule the maritime provinces was foiled.

For over 60 years, from the time of King Vimaladharmasūrya II (1684–1706 A.C.) to King Śrī Vijaya Rājasiṃha (1739–1747 A.C.), there was peace and tranquility in the country. There were no noteworthy internal feuds nor were the Sinhalese at war with the Dutch. As a result, this period is marked with some development in the religion and literature as well as the economic conditions of the country. The whole of the reign of King Rājasiṃha II was taken up with warfare and he had no time to do anything for the advancement of either the country or the religion. Consequently, the religion deteriorated. As has been noted previously, it was difficult to find even five virtuous *bhikkhus* who had received higher ordination. Therefore, King Vimaladharmasūrya II, like his predecessor, dispatched ambassadors to Arakan where he obtained thirty-three *bhikkhus* and re-established higher ordination in Ceylon.

However, foreign domination, and consequent political and economic weaknesses together with corruption prevented Buddhism from retaining its original purity. Monks led a loose, irreligious life that was useless to themselves as well as to the country. They were, by and large, uneducated. They engaged themselves in agriculture, medicine, fortune telling, and even raised and supported families. The life of the layman was even more pitiful. There was no initiative whatsoever for the liberation and the development of the country.

At this time there appeared on the scene a young novice (*sāmaṇera*) named Välivița Piṇḍapātika Saraṇaṃkara, dynamic in thought and action. Intent on producing a group of high-quality citizens for the liberation of the land and its religion, he embarked on a plan to educate and improve the moral state of the country.

The degree of degeneration to which the nation had sunk at this time is clearly evidenced by the opposition brought to bear against this well intentioned and noble religio-national rejuvenation movement of the Ven. Saraṇaṃkara.

"All the *sāmaṇeras* (novice monks) in the temples of the Kandy District as well as all other monks were jealous. They opposed and obstructed those monks who lived according to precepts."[1] Not only the chief monks of temples, but also the chieftains and the king himself were opposed to this new movement at the beginning. Nevertheless, in the face of these odds, patiently and resolutely, Välivița Piṇḍapātika Saraṇaṃkara was able to revive Buddhism, national pride, culture, and literature. King Kīrti Śrī Rājasiṃha (1747–1798 A.C.), pleased with the Ven. Saraṇaṃkara's venture, sent ambassadors to Siam in 1750 with instructions to bring some *bhikkhus* to Ceylon. The ambassadors returned with a group of *bhikkhus* headed by Upāli Mahā Thera, whereupon the king re-established the pure higher ordination and appointed the Ven. Välivița Piṇḍapātika Saraṇaṃkara as the *Sangha Rāja* (king of *bhikkhus*) of Ceylon.

The Dutch strengthened their maritime fortresses and began a gradual infiltration into the interior of the country. King Kīrti Śrī Rājasiṃha made a valiant effort to drive them away. Under Dutch rule, just as under the Portuguese, the culture and moral tone of the people, their economic and political progress, all suffered immeasurable losses and deprivation. As a result of the alarmingly heavy taxes imposed by the greedy governors, the country was pauperized. The Dutch monopolized the trade in cinnamon, coffee, and areca nuts. The cinnamon trade was practically a state monopoly. People were even prohibited from peeling cinnamon plants that grew in their own gardens. The Dutch did little for the development of the provinces they ruled.

More than anything else, the Dutch were anxious to propagate Protestantism in Ceylon. They built churches in all districts which they ruled and opened schools in villages. Books on Christianity were printed and published in the Sinhala and Tamil languages. Only those who embraced Christianity were appointed as teachers in their schools. They served not only as teachers but also as registrars of marriages and had the power to baptize. The villagers therefore respected them and as a mark of this respect they addressed them as *Rāḷahāmi* (an honorific title). At one time the teacher in a church in Colombo was invested with the high title of *Mudaliyar*. The law demanded that all children should be sent to Christian schools for their education.

Those who were not officially Protestants could obtain no office in the government. It became essential that one should convert even to be appointed a very minor functionary in a village. Many Buddhists embraced Protestantism for no other reason than that of obtaining employment.

In this manner the Dutch attempted to replace Buddhism with Christianity, the Sinhala-Buddhist culture with the alien Christian culture and to stabilize their power by destroying the respect, love, and loyalty of the Sinhala people for their king and country. The Dutch ruled the maritime provinces of Ceylon for 138 long years, from 1658–1796.

While Sinhala culture and Buddhism were being thus

crippled and suppressed, facing near extinction in the coastal areas, the Buddhist monks, to the best of their ability in these circumstances, continued teaching Buddhism and literature to village children in the remote, rural parts of the country, in a desperate attempt to save religion and culture.

13. BRITISH RULE

It is probable that the English first planned the conquest of Ceylon in 1763. By this time Calcutta, Bombay, and Madras in the Indian sub-continent were occupied by the British. In 1763 the English governor of Madras sent an envoy named Phybus to King Kīrti Śrī Rājasiṃha in Kandy, expressing his willingness to support the king and fight the Dutch. Though the envoy returned to Madras with a draft agreement after his meeting and discussions with the king, Kīrti Śrī Rājasiṃha received no assistance whatsoever from the British in Madras.

Nevertheless, in 1782, Lord McCartney, Governor of Madras, dispatched troops with a British fleet to Ceylon, with the intention of capturing the maritime provinces occupied by the Dutch. They captured the fortress at Trincomalee. An effort on the part of the English to enter into a fresh treaty with the Sinhala king at this stage proved a failure, for Kīrti Śrī Rājasiṃha had lost faith in the British who had ignored the earlier plan. However, as the result of a peace treaty in Europe in 1783, the fortress at Trincomalee was restored to the Dutch.

War in Europe again aroused hostilities between the British and the Dutch in 1795. In this year Lord Hobart, Governor of Madras, sent an army to Ceylon and captured the fortress at Trincomalee. A month later the British captured Jaffna. In the following month Negombo fell. On February 16, 1796, the British conquered the fort of Colombo and ended Dutch rule in Ceylon.

From 1796 the British ruled over all those territories previously held by the Dutch. The British, like their Portuguese and Dutch predecessors, did everything possible to undermine Buddhism and Sinhala culture, to spread Christianity and western culture, to create disaffection in the minds of the people towards their national government and to strengthen the power of their own government in Ceylon. They aimed at gaining supremacy over the whole island by instigating internal conflicts among the Sinhalese. The Sinhalese and the British often quarreled and, in 1803, the British declared war on the Sinhala king. Thenceforth, the British harnessed all their might and strength to destroy the Sinhala monarchy.

The freedom of the Sinhala nation and the freedom of Buddhism in Ceylon were lost to the British on March 2, 1815, in Kandy. Thus the British became the first and the only foreign power in history to occupy the whole of Ceylon.

Even on this darkest and saddest day in the history of the Sinhala nation, even in the deeply depressing last moment of their freedom, the honor and prestige of the proud Sinhalese and their religion was saved and protected by a *bhikkhu.*

Until the Kandyan Convention was accepted and signed that day by both parties, in the Audience Hall in Kandy, the British had no lawful right or authority to hoist their flag in Kandy. An impatient British soldier, elated with a sense of victory and being more than sure that in a few more minutes the flag of his nation was destined to flutter victoriously in the cool breeze of the Kandyan hills, regardless of whether his action was lawful or not, hoisted the Union Jack, even before the Convention was signed. In that august gathering that day there was not a single self-respecting, brave Sinhalese layman who had the courage to stand up against this humiliation to nation and religion, both of which had enjoyed the fruits of freedom for more than two thousand years.

But at that moment, when the last breath of freedom was being extinguished, at that gloomy ceremony where the death knell of a free nation was about to be sounded, the Ven. Vāriyapoḷa Vinayācārya Dīpaṃkara Anu-Nāyaka Thera of the Huduhumpoḷa Royal Temple[1] in Kandy who was present at this meeting, inspired by the pride of his nation and impelled by the love and devotion to his religion, surged out of the crowd, pushed away the British soldier, tore down the Union Jack, trampled on it and standing upon it said in a voice fearless and resonant: "Until the Convention is complete this flag cannot be hoisted here." Even today a reminiscence of this deed of Vāriyapoḷa Thera acts as a divine spell to inspire the Sinhala people with national pride.

It is clear therefore, that from the beginning to the end of the history of the Sinhala nation, *bhikkhus* were the custodians of its freedom, culture and civilization, literature, arts, and crafts. On every occasion when both the nation and the religion were in danger, Buddhist monks came forward to save and protect them. Because of this selflessness and because of the services rendered by the *bhikkhu,* people listened to his words with love and respect.

14. STRUGGLE FOR FREEDOM: REBELLIONS

The Sinhalese detested living under British subjugation. *Bhikkhus* abhorred it particularly because it was both a non-Buddhist and a foreign government. On several occasions patriotic Sinhalese rebelled against the British with the noble intention of liberating their country and religion. These rebellions were usually inaugurated under the leadership of *bhikkhus*. The rebellion of 1818, which spread throughout the Kandyan Districts, was indeed headed by *bhikkhus*. L. A. Mills categorically says that *bhikkhus* opposed the British Government and that therefore they took the lead in organizing the rebellion of 1818.[1]

The rebellion of 1834 also began with the assistance of Buddhist monks. In 1843 another rebellion developed under the leadership of a *thera* named Chandajoti.[2]

In 1848 there was a new revolt against the British. In a letter to the Chief Secretary in Colombo, written in 1848 by John S. Colepepper, it was stated that this revolt, too, was headed by *bhikkhus*.[3] To this day it is popularly known among the elderly people in the Daṁbulla area that the Ven. Girānegama Chandajoti Nāyaka Thera of the Daṁbulla Rock Temple acted as the leader for the Daṁbulla district in this revolt. Nine other monks of the Daṁbulla district were arrested in this revolt.[4]

A *thera* known as Kuḍāpola was questioned by the English about the rebellion. He was unable to give any information, was indicted, and sentenced to be shot. H. C. Selby, K.C., appealed to the governor, Viscount Torrington, to change the sentence, pointing out that there was no evidence even for a charge against this *bhikkhu,* let alone the death penalty imposed on him. Nevertheless, Governor Viscount Torrington, regardless of all the claims of justice, had this Buddhist monk shot dead in his yellow robes. Furthermore, this governor caused several hundreds of other people to be executed. The Chief Justice of the time threatened to resign in protest against these cruelties. The atrocities of Viscount Torrington were of such magnitude that the British Government recalled him.[5]

Thus, even in the 19th century, as in the past, patriotic Sinhalese laymen and the clergy fought together, sacrificing their lives in the cause of freedom and religion. Whatever the results of their efforts, whether successful or not, the Sinhala nation is forever beholden to these noble heroes.

15. THE STRENGTH OF THE *BHIKKHUS*: LAY-CLERGY UNITY

Examining and analyzing the rebellions of the Sinhala people for their freedom, after they had been subjugated, the English learned some valuable lessons. They discovered that the unity and solidarity of the Sinhala nation consisted of the close relationship and identification between the laity and the *Sangha;* that the *bhikkhus* were leaders and freedom-fighters in their rebellions against British rule; and that the unity between the laity and the *Sangha* had to be destroyed if the country was to be governed peacefully and without interruption.

A letter dated February 27, 1805, sent by Governor Frederick North to Lord Camden in England says: "The influence of Candy (i.e. Kandyan Kingdom) in these Settlements is founded on Buddhism."[1] In another letter written in January 1807 by Governor Maitland to Eden, the Government Agent of the Mātara district, the governor says: "The influence of the Priests is very great, even greater in many instances than that of the Modeliars (i.e. *mudaliyars*) themselves."

Insight into the unity between the laity and the *Sangha* and the influence of *bhikkhus* in the 19th century is provided by a report written by the Commissioners of the *vihāra* and *devāla* lands.

> Besides the relation in which the priests stand to their tenants as landlords, and the religious influence

> of their possession, they have other holds on the affection of the people. Their *pansalas* are the schools for village children, and the sons of even the superior head-men are very generally educated at them.[2] They have also, frequently, some knowledge of medicine, and when this is the case they generally give the benefit of their advice gratuitously,[3] which the *vedaralas*[4] seldom do. Add to this that, as every revenue officer who has ever attempted to induce the natives to exert themselves for their own good knows, the priests are generally, when properly applied to, foremost with their money, if rich, or with their influence or both, in furthering every scheme, for local improvement; and from what has been stated, it will be evident that not only is it their interest to be kind and considerate to their tenants, but that they generally are so, and that their influence among the people is, in a social point of view, usefully employed. (Quoted from S. T. Report, 1872, p. 448)[5]

Robert Percival gives the following account of the position of the *bhikkhus* in 19th century society in the Kandyan Kingdom:

> The priests of Buddou (i.e. Buddha) are in Ceylon accounted superior to all others. They are called Tirinanxes (i.e. *terunnānsēs*) and are held in high estimation at the Court of Candy (i.e. Kandy), where indeed they have the chief management of affairs. The King has no authority over them, but endeavours to get their good will by respecting their immunities, and loading them with distinctions. They have on many occasions shown their gratitude for these attentions, and have materially assisted him both in repressing disturbances in his own dominions and by exciting the people to support him in his wars against the Dutch . . . .

In such high veneration are the Tirinanxes held that their persons are accounted sacred, and the King of Candy, absolute as he is, has no power to take away their lives or anywise punish them even for conspiring against his own life. They chuse their Superiors; and their Chief Priest or archbishop is vested with the power of settling all religious disputes. The body of Tirinanxes are elected by the King from among the nobles, and they are consequently men possessed of power and influence even independent of their sacred character.[6]

16. BRITISH TACTICS: DISRUPTION OF LAY-CLERGY UNITY

The British clearly understood that *bhikkhus* should be isolated from society and social service activities in order to destroy the influence they held over the people and that the strong lay-clergy bond of unity and fidelity should be broken if they were to govern the country peacefully.[1] The tactics adopted by them to achieve this end are now known to us from secret British memoranda.

Some of the leading monks who wielded considerable influence over the people were invested with honors and titles and offices to win their favor and enlist their loyalty. This created jealousies and conflicts among the chief monks themselves as well as a rift between the Buddhist monks and the leading laymen.

Here is just one illustration of the tactics adopted by the English to achieve their aim. At that time there lived in the Mātara district two venerable *theras,* Karatoṭa Thera and Bōvala Thera, both very powerful and influential. The Ven. Bōvala Thera commanded enormous public support. Governor Maitland, who realized that the strength of Bōvala Thera was an obstacle to the English Government, attempted to undermine his position through Karatoṭa Thera. So the governor prepared to win over the Ven. Karatoṭa by appointing him high priest (*nāyaka thera*) and thereafter involving him in intrigue against the *mudaliyars* and other leaders, both lay and clergy.

This piece of cunning is clear from a letter written in January 1807 by Governor Maitland to Eden, the Government Agent of the Mātara district:

> Independent however of the Policy I wish to observe with regard to the Modaliars and by a cautious adherence to which you will acquire a more thoro' knowledge of your district than has hitherto been obtained, you have too another Engine in your hands; but the management of which will require extreme caution, prudence, and above all secrecy.
>
> It applies to the religion and prejudices of the Cingalese in the district of Matura and will require considerable explanation:
>
> It is my intension to appoint a committee of Buddhoo Priests to whom all cases which occur in your Province, relative either to the Priests themselves, or their lands and their religious ceremonies, are to be referred to for decision; my object in forming this sort of Committee is first to convince the people that the greatest respect and attention shall be shown to their religious prejudices and customs; secondly to give the priests themselves a fellow feeling with our Government, and of course an interest in supporting its authority among the inhabitants, and thereby to break through the Powerful combination which has hitherto, from want of taking a proper view of the subject, been allowed to subsist between the Modeliars and the Principal Priests to the great detriment of the British Interest, and obvious advantage of the King of Kandy.
>
> In order to enable you to promote the object which I have in view, I shall give you a short account of the institutions of the Priests, of the character of the men who take the lead amongst them, of the intrigues which are kept up between them and the Modeliars,

and of the means which you must adopt to counteract them . . . .

The influence of the Priests is very great, even greater in many instances than that of the Modeliars themselves, who altho' they pretend to be Christians in consequence of a Dutch regulation, that none but natives of the Reformed Religion should hold the office of Modeliar, are to a man, worshippers of Buddhoo, and totally indifferent to Christianity . . . .[2]

The Priests who officiate in the temple (i.e. Mookirigala) have prodigious influence in the country, and the Dutch Government frequently experienced the effects of it in your Province. It is a political engine which the King of Kandi is constantly endeavouring to keep in his favour, and one which we aught by good management, to turn to our own advantage.[3] You must therefore do everything you can to cultivate the friendship, and gain the confidence of the Priests of that Temple.

Your best way of doing so will be going to the place itself and explaining to the Priests most distinctly that the Government is determined not only to tolerate but to support them in the execution of their religion and to bestow such honours, as are most congenial to their feelings upon all those who are distinguished by the extent of their learning and the propriety of their conduct;[4] let it also be clearly understood by them, that all applications they have to make must be made direct to Government thro' you and that neither the Maha nor any other Modeliar can do them any Benefit or any injury with the present government . . . .[5]

One of the great objects of Caratotte Tiroon Wahansa is to be vested by Government with some office which will give him considerable power over the Priests of his Province. He was very anxious to be appointed High Priest of Matura and Galle, as soon as he heard that I had some idea of introducing that sort of appointment . . . .

As soon as you perceive that Caratotte is willing to support Government and is completely independent of any of the Modeliars, you may hold out to him the great probability of his being appointed High Priest.[6]

But I cannot impress upon you too strongly that you must observe the greatest caution and secrecy in every step which you take relative to the Priests; in proportion as you gain them to the interests of the Government, you will diminish the influence of the Modeliars and you must therefore expect that the Modeliars will exert themselves to receive you in every point which is likely to convince the Priests of the good intentions of the Government towards them.

This letter makes it quite clear that the motive of placating the popular and powerful *bhikkhus* with high priesthoods and other such honors and offices and the appointment of *bhikkhu* committees to settle disputes among them was none other than that of cheating the *bhikkhus,* buying their loyalty to the English Government, and creating a gulf between the leading laymen and the influential Buddhist monks.

In a letter dated September 20, 1806, sent to William Windham in England, the same Governor Maitland spoke of a proposed regulation to control the *bhikkhus* in the maritime provinces and to destroy their loyalty to the Sinhala kingdom in Kandy. He writes: ". . . and now I am endeavouring to frame a Regulation which I have submitted to the Buddhoo Priests, and which they highly approve of; that will ultimately give us a preponderance over the King of Candy . . . ."[7]

It is clear that the proposed regulation was not in the least actuated by any love or consideration for the

Sinhala people or for their religion. Its sole aim was to wean the loyalty of the *bhikkhus* from the Kandyan Kingdom to the English Government of the maritime provinces.

Since the cooperation of the *bhikkhus* was essential for the continuation of the English Government in Ceylon, the latter employed many devices to gain their favor. They considered it highly significant to win their goodwill. About a month after the signing of the Kandyan Convention, on April 1, 1815, Governor Brownrigg in a dispatch to Lord Bathurst, the Secretary of State for the Colonies, wrote:

> The attendance of the Priests of the two great Temples of Kandy[8] at the Hall of Audience in the Palace on the 10th of March[9] as stated in the Bulletin of the proceedings of that day was an event of much interest and closely connected with the satisfactory issue of the Negotiations. A very slight attention to the particulars of this part of the Conference will discover how much depended on our being able to satisfy the Priesthood, and that every concession to their prejudices was a material step towards the confidence of the Chiefs and People.

In spite of all these efforts, the English still could not win over the *bhikkhus*. Whenever the opportunity arose they acted against the alien, non-Buddhist government. Therefore, it was decided to extract a pledge of loyalty to the English Government, through an Act of Appointment, from those *bhikkhus* who received conferment of high priesthood from the two Chapters of Malvatta and Asgiriya in Kandy. This is an event the significance of which should clearly be understood.

The reader will remember that the Ven. Kuḍāpoḷa

Thera was unjustly executed in his robes on the orders of Governor Viscount Torrington. The governor was a man who tried to suppress *bhikkhus* and Buddhism. It was absolutely necessary for the English to keep *bhikkhus* "loyal and faithful" to the government, and to get them to spy on those ill-disposed towards it. Torrington decided that the best way to achieve this goal was to get those *bhikkhus* who received their Act of Appointment to high priesthood to enter into some sort of agreement or promise that they would remain loyal and faithful to the English Government and supply the government with information. Thus, an Act of Appointment was devised and drafted incorporating the statements that the high priesthood was conferred by virtue of the powers vested by Viscount Torrington, that the recipient *bhikkhu* should remain loyal and faithful to the English Government and should be vigilant against those acts of treason or betrayal, and inform the Government of people opposed to it. An extract from the Act of Appointment usually granted by the Malvatta Chapter in Kandy will illustrate this point more clearly.

> Since His Excellency the Governor Viscount Torrington has, on the 22nd day of the month of July in the year 1847 of the Christian Era at the Royal Palace in Senkaḍagala Mahanuvara (Kandy), transferred to us the power exercised by the Government with regard to the religion, stating that the Government had no objection whatever to our exercising all those powers and privileges continued from ancient times concerning Buddhism, by that power . . . .[10]

What is evident from the above statement is that conferment of high priesthood is carried out not by the power or authority of the Council of the *Sangha* (*Saṅgha*

Sabhā) but by the power vested in himself by the non-Buddhist governor.

The exhortation of the chief high priest (*mahā nāyaka thera*) to a newly appointed high priest is also stated in this Act of Appointment, which begins: ". . . therefore you, Ven. High Priest, being loyal and faithful to the Exalted English Government and to our Council of the *Mahā Saṅgha* . . . ."

It should be noted that a high priest has to be loyal and faithful not only to the Council of the *Mahā Saṅgha* but also to the "Exalted English Government." And, furthermore, it continues: ". . . if any one of the *bhikkhus* belonging to the Fraternity of our *vihāra,* resident in the said [your] district, were to do or utter things against the Exalted English Government and against the traditions of our religion; any treasonable, crafty, and treacherous meetings; when such a situation comes to your knowledge, you must completely investigate it and you must as soon as possible duly bring it to the notice of the Government and ourselves."

It is quite clear from this that those *mahā theras* who obtained high priesthood appointments from the Kandy Chapter were bound by a "Deed of Promise" to act as spies on their own nation.[11]

Unfortunately, many people do not realize the extent of the humiliation suffered by the *bhikkhus* and Buddhism by this Act, nor do they understand that the members of the *Saṅgha Sabhā* in Kandy disgraced themselves and their religion.

Among the functions relating to the execution of the law, that of the hangman may perhaps be considered as the lowest and the most despicable. Similarly, among political activities, spying may perhaps be considered the most degrading. Could there be anything more degenerate, more disgraceful, and more debased than to be a spy on one's own nation for an alien government, which is the case of our *nāyaka theras*—whom we honor and respect—our *nāyaka theras* who became spies by accepting the office of high priest conferred on them by the same Viscount Torrington who had the Ven. Kuḍāpoḷa shot in his yellow robes?

It is evident from history that these *bhikkhus* fell into this depth of degeneration on account of the machinations of the English Government. This Act of Appointment was certainly drafted on the orders of Governor Viscount Torrington and incorporated his ideas.

This corrupt Act of Appointment, so treacherously worded, has been handed down during the past one hundred years by the two Chapters of Malvatta and Asgiriya in Kandy. Perhaps they might have continued doing this unthinkingly not realizing, perhaps, the gravity and implications of their action. But now it is time to revise this Act of Appointment, removing from it those disgraceful phrases which call for the betrayal of the nation and the religion, and to remodel it in order to protect and preserve the dignity and prestige of the Sinhala nation and the Buddhist religion. That will be a historic step towards national and religious freedom.

If this is not done the Chapters will earn the approbrium of future generations.[12]

17. BRITISH TACTICS: CONFUSION OF MONASTIC ADMINISTRATION

While attempting to win over the leading Buddhist monks by tempting and deceiving them with honors, the English maneuvered yet again to disrupt and confuse Buddhist activities. This was done by severing the Government's connections with the administration of Buddhist temporalities.

In a previous chapter it was pointed out that Buddhist activities were well and smoothly conducted during the time of the ancient Sinhala kings, because Buddhist temporalities were properly managed and administered by a department established within the government.

In keeping with this ancient custom, according to Article 5 of the Kandyan Convention of 1815, it was the duty and the responsibility of the British Government to maintain and protect "the Religion of Boodhoo" and its rites, ministers, and places of worship. Nevertheless, Christian missionaries strongly objected to the British Government—a Christian government—condoning Buddhist activities. Accordingly the British Government severed all of its connections with those activities. Of this L. A. Mills says:

> A new phase of the Buddhist question developed in the 'forties, owing to the hostilities of the Ceylon missionaries and their powerful adherents in Great Britain to the British Government's connection with "idolatry." They objected especially to the appoint-

> ment of priests by the governor, and demanded a complete severance of relations between church and state. Carried away by religious scruples, Governor Mackenzie in 1840 refused to sign the warrants appointing priests to the chief temples, because to do so was a "direct encouragement to" Buddhism . . . .[1]
>
> In November 1844, Lord Stanley, the Secretary of State of the Colonies, was won over by the missionaries and instructed the governor to sever all connection with Buddhism . . . .
>
> In 1847 Governor Torrington resigned Buddha's Tooth to the custody of the priests, discontinued the annual allowance of £300 made towards the cost of the temple rites, and informed the priesthood that the government's decision to sever all connections with Buddhism was irrevocable.[2]

The missionaries and the British Government were successful in their intentions. From 1840, the year in which Governor Mackenzie refused to sign the warrants appointing priests to the chief temples, the administration of Buddhist temporalities became more and more confused. From that time tenants living on temple lands ignored paying the share of revenue that belonged to the temples. In the absence of any legal power either to appoint or to dismiss a lay trustee, some laymen misappropriated and enjoyed revenues that belonged to the temples. Courts of Law were reluctant to entertain a complaint from a *bhikkhu* until he could legally prove that he was the chief incumbent of the temple—often a difficult task.[3] As there was no legal means of collecting and controlling the revenues of the temple lands, the confusion in Buddhist activities was doubly confounded. On the one hand the lay trustees and the tenants misappropriated monastic revenue, and on the other hand the *bhikkhus* themselves began to use temporalities improperly according to their individual whims and fancies. Some began to support their relatives with temple revenues, while others even maintained families. It is reported that the character and integrity of the *bhikkhus* were highly exemplary around the period of the Kandyan Convention.[4] But along with the confusion brought about by the administration of Buddhist temporalities, the conduct of the *bhikkhus* too became reprehensible. This caused great damage to the peaceful harmony and unity that existed between laymen and *bhikkhus,* inevitably paving the way for the deterioration of Buddhist activities and the decline of Buddhism.

18. BRITISH TACTICS: INTRIGUES TO DESTROY BUDDHISM (CHRISTIAN EDUCATION)

Thus, while winning over the leading *bhikkhus* and undermining the administration of Buddhist temporalities, the British adopted another line of activity to destroy Buddhism and Sinhala national culture.

The reader will recollect that during the time of the Sinhala Kingdom the entire education of the country—the education of all children from prince to peasant's son—was free and given by the temple, and that as a result there existed an inseparable and strong bond between laymen and *bhikkhus*. This was the secret of the security and the development of the nation and the religion. And it was because of the strength of this bond that the Sinhala people were always able to rise up against any foreign ruler.

If the British administration in Ceylon was to continue uninterrupted and steady, it was necessary, as a first principle of political strategy, to destroy this strength and to replace it with Christian strength. The British administrators who realized this, while doing everything possible within their power to enfeeble Buddhism, imported Christian missionaries from Europe, paid them salaries from state revenues,[1] opened Christian schools, spread Christianity with western culture, converted Buddhist children to Christianity and taught them that their Sinhalese Buddhist culture was low and inferior, and a thing to be despised. All this helped to widen the gulf between laymen and *bhikkhus*, to destroy their unity and sap their strength.

A letter dated February 27, 1805, written by Governor Fredrick North to Lord Camden in England refers to three Christian ministers who had arrived in Ceylon. The services of these ministers, it is stated, were extremely valuable, not only from the point of view of religion but politically too.

In a letter to Lord Castlereagh, Governor Maitland wrote on March 11, 1809: "To the various sects of Christians I have ever extended the Protection of the Government on every instance. To the others I have extended merely that species of Protection which admitted of their following without the Interference of Government their own Faith."[2]

A letter dated March 3, 1821, sent by Governor Edward Barnes to Lord Bathurst, mentions that 2,000 rixdollars had been loaned to a certain Christian society by the Government for the translation of the Bible into Sinhala. A footnote in the same letter indicates that this loan was not recalled; instead, sometime afterwards, it was considered as a donation.

Article 5 of the Kandyan Convention of March 2, 1815, reads: "The Religion of Boodhoo . . . is declared inviolable, and its Rites, Ministers, and Places of worship are to be maintained and protected."

The meaning of this Article is self-evident: The British Government undertakes to maintain and protect Buddhism, Buddhist monks, and Buddhist temples. Governor Sir Robert Brownrigg signed this Convention for and on behalf of the British Government.

The correspondence exchanged between Governor Brownrigg and the Secretary of State for the Colonies in regard to this Article of the Convention appears to be voluminous. And these letters reveal the concerted secret efforts of the British Government to destroy Buddhism in spite of its pledge and to spread Christianity in its place. A few excerpts from some of these letters are reproduced in these pages for the information of the reader.

In a letter of March 15, 1815, (i.e. 13 days after the Kandyan Convention), addressed to Lord Bathurst, Secretary of State for the Colonies, Governor Sir Robert Brownrigg, who signed the Convention, in the course of explaining it, says about the 5th Article:

> The 5th confirms the Superstition of Boodhoo[3] in a manner more Emphatical than would have been my choice. But the Reverence felt towards it at present by all classes of the Inhabitants is unbounded and mixed with a strong shade of jealousy, and doubt about its future protection—and that in truth our secure possession of the Country hinged upon this point. I found it necessary to quiet all uneasiness respecting it, by an article of guarantee couched in the most unqualified terms.

The Secretary of State for the Colonies criticized the governor for the 5th Article of the Convention. Governor Brownrigg defended his position in the following extracts from a letter dated June 1, 1816, to Bathurst:

> My Lord . . . . Among the various points of great interest which occupy Your Lordship's remark on the Act of Convention, my earliest and most anxious attention is due to the doubt which arose on the first impression of the term *inviolable* used in the fifth Article as applicable to the superstition of Boodhoo. I greatly lament that anything under my sanction

should have generated even a momentary idea, that I could possibly have overlooked or neglected the strong and reiterated injunction, by which the dissemination of Christian knowledge is recommended to my support, in the Instructions and Despatches under which I have the honor to represent His Majesty's Government here. I venture to hope that the justice Your Lordship has done to the term in question, by construing it from the context, will relieve the Convention from the Odium which would rightly attach to it, if the emancipation of the Kandyan Kingdom and People, however otherwise laudable, were connected with any compromise of the Interests of the Christian Faith.

Perhaps I might hope that my Administration of the Government of this Colony has not been of a character to found the supposition, that I should have been indifferent to the propagation of the Gospel, and still less calculated I trust to give countenance to that construction of a doubtful expression, which would impute to me the deliberate act of barring the introduction of Christianity into a country which I have been the humble instrument of annexing to His Majesty's Dominion.

The affirmative part of the clause namely "that the Rites, Ministers, and places of the Boodhoo worship are to be maintained and protected" embraces (as Your Lordship has justly construed it) the sum total of support engaged for on the part of the British Government and the negative term inviolable I can affirm to Your Lordship never to have had greater latitude of acceptation in my mind, than that the Budha Religion should not be abolished or obstructed.

I am so far from considering the Kandyan People as permanently debarred from the light of Christianity, that I think it requires no great share of foresight to predict, that the gloom of ignorance and Superstition which has hitherto enveloped that unfortunate region, will at no distant period be materially dissipated, by the gradual and insensible diffusion of religious knowledge, so that a safe and promising trial may be made of a direct appeal to the reason of the people, for their own happiness, and the honour of that faith which in due time will be universal.

That this period is not yet arrived with respect to the Kandyan Provinces, I am obliged in candour to state; but must beg leave to add that the realization of such a hope, if I should be spared even to hear of it, at whatever distance I may be placed, will impart to my mind a satisfaction beyond any other which I can expect this life to afford.

Further, in a letter dated June 13, 1816, written by Governor Brownrigg to William Wilberforce in England, he gives a detailed description of the various steps taken by him to eradicate Buddhism and also the means adopted to spread Christianity.

Dear Sir,

I have very lately received in an Enclosure from my friend Sir Henry Calvert, a Letter of yours addressed to Him upon the Subject of an Article in the Convention, by which the Dominion of the Kandyan Provinces was vested in the Sovereign of the British Empire.

I cannot disguise the pain and mortification I have felt, upon learning that such an erroneous interpretation as you describe should have been given to that Treaty, and that from one single Word inferences should have been drawn in direct contradiction to the whole tenour of those principles upon which my government of this Island has been invariably conducted.

I am however much gratified and consoled by the manner in which you have communicated this painful intelligence; for I see that you have yourself put the just and liberal construction upon my Words, and you offer me through the medium of your Correspondence the most effective method of removing a misconception so injurious to my Character.

I with pleasure avail myself of your desire I should see your Letter to Sir Henry Calvert, and consider as an invitation to address my Answer directly to yourself.

I reflect also now with much satisfaction upon having even this Correspondence by a Letter which I did myself the honour to write to you on the 22nd of last July, upon the Subject of our Religious progress in the Island.

No part of the Statement you have heard has given me such astonishment as that in which it is said that what is termed the Anti-Christian sense of the Word "inviolable," has been attached to it in this Island.

The term was certainly strong, and although nothing more was meant by it than a complete security from any kind of Violence to the Budha worship, and a full protection to their religious property; yet if it has been misunderstood anywhere, I sincerely regret that it was ever adopted.

But assuredly the last place in which I expected to hear of such a misconception was the Island of Ceylon.

I have been here now more than four years and I may venture to assert without fear of contradiction that the chief object of my Government has been the Religious and moral improvement of People, and the propagation of the Gospel . . . .

It has been a matter of peculiar satisfaction to me that I have seen under my Government, Wesleyans, Presbyterians, and Baptists, uniting with the regular Clergy of the Church of England, in Preaching the Gospel of our Saviour—Can it be supposed that when a New Field was open for propagating our Holy Religion, I should at once bar the Gate against the introduction of the Christian Faith, that in any part of this Island Christianity should alone be deprived of a right to toleration and that I should stipulate not for protection of Budha but exclusion of Christ? Be assured, My Dear Sir, I have never entered into such a strange engagement, nor was any Article in the Kandyan Convention ever so understood by either of the contracting Parties. The word "inviolable" has been rendered into Cingalese by a Phrase signifying literally "not to be broken down" and so the Kandyans clearly received the clause; they considered that I had covenanted not to break down, i.e., to overturn their Religion. I have already informed them of my intension to establish a School for teaching English in Kandy, and they have given their decided approbation to the measure.

I believe at present the most sanguine Missionaries in India consider that instructing the Native Youth is the surest means of spreading the Gospel.

I have heard no proposal yet from any Missionary to go into the Kandyan Provinces, and to say the truth, I believe that there is no part of India where at present a Mission would in all likelihood be more unpromising . . . .

The good understanding at present between our Countrymen and the Kandyans, will it is to be hoped at no distant period, lead to an opening for great Religious and Moral improvement, in a Country which has for ages been consigned to barbarous ignorance. But hasty or injudicious attempts at the Commencement of our friendly Connection, might do serious Mischief, and much retard the great Work of Conversion.

If ever there was a Situation in which a political Union with a New and Strange people, demanded caution and descretion in adopting measures likely to offend their prejudices and Superstition, my present relation to the Kandyan Nation assuredly requires circumspection and caution (prudence?).

If I appear at first slow in my efforts I entreat you to believe that I am not the less sincere in my desire to see the blessings of Christianity diffused among the lately acquired subjects of Great Britain.

It is not that my zeal for the propagation of the Gospel has abated but the peculiar circumstances of the case compel me to deliberate upon the steps that I am to take. But if the general character of the Kandyans is at present unfavourable to missionary operations, there is one superstitious notion prevalent among them of promising nature. It is currently received that there existed a close connection between the independence of the Kandyan Kingdom and the reign of Budhism. Budha it is believed engaged to protect their Monarchy against all foreign power or influence; but they are now become the subjects of an European Prince, the promise is violated and the reliance upon Budha is at an end.

I do indeed, My Dear Sir, look forward with anxious hope to the time, when after a mutual Confidence has been cemented between the British Government and our Kandyan Subjects, a better system of Education, and an effectual Introduction of the Gospel, will produce the downfall of Budhist Superstition, and of the still more vile and degrading Idolatry of Demon Worship.

This should reveal to the reader how the British Government tried to destroy Buddhism and Buddhist culture in Ceylon and to spread Christianity and western culture in its place. The reader can now understand that the pledge to maintain and protect Buddhism given by the British was, in effect, farcical.

19. NATIONAL AND RELIGIOUS DEGENERATION

So, in the manner described earlier, with missionaries imported from foreign countries with government assistance, schools were opened in different parts of the country. Through these schools the British Government began to spread Christianity and western culture and convert Buddhists to Christianity. All social and welfare activities hitherto undertaken by *bhikkhus* fell into the hands of these missionaries, and their power loomed large. Because of the privileged position of the missionaries, their help and assistance were sought. The intervention of the missionaries was necessary even to secure employment. A certificate issued by a missionary was respected by the Government. Moreover, the Government favored Christians. A Buddhist had no place in the higher strata of society. He did not belong to the elite. Therefore, for the sake of materialistic gains, many Sinhalese embraced Christianity. Buddhists were reluctant to profess their faith in public places such as the Law Courts and the Kachcheries.

Foreign missionaries taught the Sinhalese children to look down upon and despise Sinhala Buddhist culture as low and base—a thing inferior—and to value and appreciate Christian culture as immeasurably superior.[1]

Those Sinhalese who forsook Buddhism and embraced Christianity despised Sinhala Buddhist habits and customs, discarded Sinhalese names and dress, and imitated western styles. They scorned the Sinhala language and looked down on Sinhalese literature as a thing of no value or significance. They were prouder of Rome or Canterbury than of Anurādhapura or Poḷonnaruva. They even began to think of England as their motherland instead of Mother Lankā, Ceylon.

It was this attitude which encouraged people, particularly the growing generation, to despise their own heritage and take up an alien culture which brought about the decline of Sinhala Buddhist culture—the foundation of the Sinhala nation. If a nation loses its own culture, it cannot hope for freedom or development; it can only expect degeneration and slavery.

With the missionaries asserting their power under the Christians, the position of the *bhikkhu* began to deteriorate. As the Buddhist monks could not adapt themselves to suit the changed political, economic, and social situation, they were rendered useless to society. Nor did they receive an education to prepare them for these new conditions. They had no plan of action. Their word was no more respected. Laymen had nothing to learn from them. Therefore, laymen—particularly those of the upper class—dissociated themselves from *bhikkhus* and the bond between the laity and the clergy declined. *Bhikkhus* lost their places and positions in society. Functions and privileges which they had enjoyed hitherto were usurped by, or fell into the hands of, the missionaries.

Thus the *bhikkhu,* circumscribed both with regard to personality and education, was by force of circumstances driven to limit his activities to the recitation of the *Suttas* (*Pirit* chanting), preaching a sermon, attendance at funeral rites and alms-givings in memory of the departed, and to an idle, cloistered life in the temple. In spite of this melancholy and abject situation into which the *bhikkhu* was forced, any remnants of Sinhala Buddhist culture in the country, particularly in the rural areas, however insignificant they might have been, had ultimately been preserved and maintained by the *bhikkhus* themselves. Whatever depths of calamity these venerable monks had sounded, whatever hardships they had to face, they never forgot that Sinhala Buddhist culture was their noblest heritage and treasure.

The reader will recall that in ancient Ceylon Buddhism and Sinhala culture were inseparable. The ancient Sinhalese could think of no national development without religion and no religious development without nation. Christian missionaries, however, taught the Sinhalese to think of national development as something apart from religious development. This was necessary for them to convert Buddhists to Christianity.

To the ancient Sinhalese Buddhism was the greatest national treasure. According to them, therefore, a Sinhalese had to be a Buddhist. The glory of the Buddhist culture and civilization of the Sinhala nation, its unity and progress, was its consequence. But from the day the Sinhalese were taught to think of the nation and the religion as things apart, unrelated to each other, they shamelessly became Christians. To a Sinhalese conversion to Christianity was a stigma. Sinhalese society looked down upon such converts.

It should be clearly understood that what the Sinhalese Buddhists opposed was not the religious teaching of Jesus of Nazareth, but a religion together with an alien civilization propagated by the imperialists as a mode of destroying patriotism and national culture and establishing foreign rule in Ceylon. In this way Christianity came to be identified with imperialism and anti-nationalism.[2]

20. THE REVIVAL

When Buddhism and the Sinhala nation had sunk into this piteously helpless situation under a non-Buddhist alien government, once again there appeared on the scene, during the 19th century, a few Buddhist monks of heroic character intent on reviving the nation and its religion. The Ven. Valānē Śrī Siddhārtha Mahā Thera, reputedly a very handsome and imposing man, regarded as the finest Buddhist scholar at that time in Ceylon, established in 1841 a monastery named Parama-dhamma-cetiyārāma at Ratmalāna, a suburb of Colombo, and founded there the Parama-dhamma-cetiya Pirivena (monastic college), both of which still flourish. Among the *bhikkhus* who studied at the Parama-dhamma-cetiya Pirivena, the center where the present revival of Buddhist learning and culture originated, were the Ven. Hikkaḍuvē Śrī Sumangala Nāyaka Thera who established, in 1873, the Vidyodaya Pirivena[1] at Māligākanda, Colombo, and the Ven. Ratmalānē Śrī Dharmāloka Mahā Thera who established, in 1875, the Vidyālaṅkāra Pirivena[2] at Pāliyagoḍa near Colombo. Through these two *pirivenas*—Vidyodaya and Vidyālaṅkāra—Sinhala literature and Buddhist culture once again received a new lease on life.

The first Buddhist school in Ceylon was opened in 1869 by the Ven. Doḍandūvē Piyaratana Tissa Nāyaka Thera, near his temple Śailabimbārāma in Doḍandūva.[3]

At this same time, the Ven. Migeṭṭuvattē Śrī Guṇānanda Thera, the Ven. Battaramullē Śrī Subhūti Thera, and the Ven. Koratoṭa Śrī Śobhita Thera led a strong anti-Christian movement to rehabilitate the honorable heritage of Buddhism. Meanwhile, in 1880, a great American, Colonel Henry Steel Olcott, arrived in Ceylon. With the assistance of the leading Buddhist monks such as Sumaṅgala, Subhūti, Piyaratana, Potuvila, Migeṭṭuvattē, and others he founded the Buddhist Theosophical Society and began opening Buddhist schools in several districts of the country. Ānanda College in Colombo, opened by Colonel Olcott in 1886, was the leading English Buddhist school.[4] Several Sinhalese such as Anagārika Dharmapāla and Brahmacārī Valisingha Harischandra made a life-long sacrifice in association with and in the cause of this program initiated by Colonel Olcott.[5]

The *bhikkhus* who completed their education in these two *pirivenas* went back to their home temples in the different parts of the country, opened new *pirivenas* affiliated to their respective *pirivenas* and embarked on the dissemination of the knowledge of the *Dhamma,* arts and sciences to both the laity and the monks for the revival of Buddhist and national culture.

Other Buddhist societies were founded on the pattern of the Buddhist Theosophical Society. The schools opened by the Buddhist Theosophical Society and other Buddhist societies enabled Sinhalese children to pursue their education free from the influence of the missionaries. The increasing number of *pirivenas* and other Buddhist schools generated a fresh enthusiasm and an interest in Buddhist culture, the Sinhala language, literature, traditions, and customs. A national reawakening was once again possible.

Nevertheless, the wealthy Sinhalese of the upper classes did not break away from their associations with the missionaries and their western Christian environment. They continued to send their children to the Christian schools; they do so even today. Those children have grown up in a foreign atmosphere, nurtured and disciplined by western habits and customs. They have no knowledge of Buddhism, Buddhist traditions and customs, the Sinhala language, literature and history. They have no regard or respect for their heritage. Though natives of Ceylon, they are more akin to foreigners in education, customs and habits, outlook, and mentality. They neither understand *bhikkhus* nor do they realize the national services performed or performable by these *bhikkhus*. Brought up according to the teachings of the missionaries, they believe that *bhikkhus* should keep out of national activities and limit themselves only to receiving alms, chanting *pirit,* performing funeral rites and preaching sermons. They believe that *bhikkhus* should live a life limited to the four walls of their temples. They do not realize that the nation and the religion have to move together.

The services rendered by the *pirivenas* from the last quarter of the 19th century have enabled Buddhist monks to develop their knowledge and education. This education, however, was not full and complete in relation to modern times. Basically, it had been limited to the ancient literature. It had been considered that modern languages and science and other modern subjects should not necessarily be taught in *pirivenas*. This was partly because the *pirivenas* had no funds and financial resources to employ teachers capable of teaching these subjects. There was no possibility of obtaining financial assistance from the Government in order to provide *bhikkhus* with a system of education in keeping with the demands of modern times.

It was undoubtedly an advantage to the British that the *bhikkhus* were exclusively devoted to the study of ancient literature, that their outlook was still the old traditional one, that they were totally ignorant of the modern world and its problems—a set of meaningless ancients living in a modern world oblivious of what was happening around them. Leading *theras* and lay Buddhist leaders, lacking vision and wisdom, objected to Buddhist monks studying English or other modern languages and subjects in the area of modern knowledge. Some of these people do not appear to have changed their attitudes even today.[6]

Because of this predicament in which the *pirivenas* were placed and in which they remain even today, it became difficult for *bhikkhus* to obtain a modern education through which they could be useful to the society in which they live. Nevertheless, certain *bhikkhus* who had a deep love of learning and of literature and a desire to contribute towards the advancement of the religion and nation made a valiant effort, in the face of many difficulties and personal hardships, to obtain the modern education which was denied to them. They continue to do so even to this day.[7]

At the present time *pirivena* education is being to some extent reorganized. But without sufficient finances no amount of structural organization will make it any more useful than it is today. Of late, the number of *bhikkhus* with *pirivena* education who enter universities continues to increase. The present generation of *bhikkhus* study not only the *Tipiṭaka,* grammar, rhetorics and prosody, but also expose themselves to a knowledge and awareness of contemporary problems through the wider media of newspapers, journals, and modern books.

A *bhikkhu* with such a knowledge of the modern

world, and of the ancient heritage of his country, aware of the problems of the day, if he is energetic and enterprising, would not like to sit idle, satiated with the sanctity afforded him within the temple precincts, devoting his life only to receive alms, chant *pirit,* perform funeral rites, and deliver the usual sermons when the country, the nation, and the religion are declining. A number of *bhikkhus* who have considered it their duty and heritage once again to liberate their country, nation, and religion, have appealed to the people of Ceylon to take up the challenge of the work in consonance with the needs of the modern world and international requirements. This is the natural process of history which cannot be stopped.

POSTSCRIPT

The first edition of this little book was published in Sinhala in 1946. Since then much has happened in Ceylon.

On February 4, 1948, Ceylon became an independent country within the Commonwealth. This was "a new façade with a burnished brass plate on the door: Free Ceylon. It was the outward and visible sign of all that the elite had been pressing for since 1910. The structure raised by the British remained intact; inside there was some rearrangement. A number of Ceylonese previously relegated to rooms without a view moved higher up; they could stride the corridors of power with more confidence and even peer out of the commanding heights of the structure. The new façade was impressive; it delighted those who filed in and out of the building as the new VIPs."[1]

Opinion was divided as to whether it was really full independence. Many Buddhist monks and laymen who believed that Buddhism, Buddhist culture, and the Sinhala language would regain their lost positions after independence were disappointed. On February 12, 1948, one week after the Declaration of Independence, the two *mahā nāyaka theras* of Asgiriya and Malvatta Chapters in Kandy wrote to Prime Minister D. S. Senanayake requesting him to include in the new Constitution the 5th Article of the Kandyan Convention which undertook to protect and safeguard Buddhism—the article which had had a notorious history. The Prime Minister, however, replied that in a country where there were several religions, Buddhism alone could not be given a special place, which indicated, in the opinion of some, that Buddhism, Buddhist culture, and the Sinhala language were in no better a position than before.

For a few wealthy, aristocratic families and their relatives and friends it was real independence, and they thoroughly enjoyed its fruits. The masses were given the opportunity to watch Independence Day celebrations in big and small towns and to listen to the patriotic speeches of the new national heroes. Little change of importance emerged to improve the social and economic conditions of the masses or to promote the national culture and heritage. Nevertheless, the Buddhists were not dismayed and enthusiasm was awakened among them for a national, cultural, and religious revival.

The movement initiated by *bhikkhus* in 1946 (see Preface to the Second Sinhala edition, above) assumed larger proportions in several ways after independence. More and more Buddhist monks were attracted to social reform and welfare activities. The Ven. Kalukoňdayāvē Paññāsekhara Mahā Nāyaka Thera led a vigorous campaign for temperance and against such social evils as gambling, drinking, and corruption. He arranged for Buddhist temples to distribute jack seeds and vegetable seeds, bread fruit and other plants among the villagers and encouraged them to produce more food. The Ven. Hīnaṭiyana Dhammāloka Nāyaka Thera directed a rural reconstruction movement, and in almost all important Buddhist temples and monasteries Rural Reconstruction Societies (*Grāmapratisaṃskaraṇa Sabhā*) under the leadership of *bhikkhus* were established. These societies even settled disputes among villagers which would otherwise have been taken to law courts.

Hīnaṭiyana, the native village of the Ven. Dhammāloka, was used as the experimental center of rural reconstruction.

In many temple premises or adjoining them, centers for medical advice and for free distribution of *āyurvedic* (indigenous) medicines were opened for the benefit of the needy. Similarly, schools for adults were conducted in temples, mainly in rural areas. Under the leadership of Buddhist monks societies were created to establish homes for the aged and orphanages, to help the poor in their need—in times of sickness and at funerals.

In 1950, the Vidyālaṅkāra Pirivena held a *saṅgāyanā,* a council of learned *theras* (elders) of all three sects in Ceylon, lasting for many months, in the fashion of the old tradition, to recite, collate, and edit the texts of the Pāli *Tipiṭaka.* This was a predecessor of the famous Sixth Council (*chaṭṭha saṅgāyanā*) in Rangoon which was organized by the Burmese Government on an enormous scale to commemorate and coincide with the 2500th anniversary of the Buddha (*Buddha Jayanti*) in 1956.

The World Fellowship of Buddhists was inaugurated in Colombo in 1950 at the initiative of Dr. G. P. Malalasekera, Professor of Pāli and Buddhist Civilization at the University of Ceylon and President of the All-Ceylon Buddhist Congress. Representatives from almost all countries in Asia and from Buddhist organizations in Europe and America attended this meeting. It was the first international Buddhist organization created for the purpose of promoting and co-ordinating Buddhist activities in different countries and bringing about understanding among them. The congress of this organization is held biennially in various countries such as

Burma, Cambodia, Ceylon, India, Japan, Nepal, and Thailand.

In April 1954, the All-Ceylon Buddhist Congress appointed a committee, the Buddhist Committee of Inquiry, consisting of seven leading Buddhist monks and nine laymen. It was created "to inquire into the present state of Buddhism in Ceylon and to report on the conditions necessary to improve and strengthen the position of Buddhism, and the means whereby those conditions may be fulfilled." It held meetings throughout the country, travelled approximately 6,300 miles, and heard evidence from organizations and individuals representing all sections of Buddhist society, both the laity and the *Sangha*. To a circulated questionnaire of 71 questions, 1,713 detailed answers were received. The Committee's report was published on February 4, 1956 (February 4th was Independence Day).

It was an important document of great interest, recapitulating the history of Buddhism in Ceylon, and of the opposition, during the previous four and a half centuries, of the foreign Christian rulers of Ceylon to Buddhism and its institutions. It made numerous recommendations touching the areas of religion and state; legislation concerning religious bodies; temporalities; establishing an incorporated body to be named the Buddha *Sāsana* Council to be in charge of Buddhist affairs; State education and taking over of assisted schools (those in receipt of State grants); the reform and reorganization of the *Sangha*; the education of *bhikkhus* and their role in social and cultural activities, among other things.

This report aroused great enthusiasm among Buddhists. Before the general election of 1956, several

Buddhist organizations, both of the *Sangha* and the laity, held public meetings and declared that they would support the party prepared to implement the recommendations of the Buddhist Committee of Inquiry.

In February 1954, at the Colombo Town Hall, the *Sinhala Jātika Sangamaya* (Sinhala National Congress), composed of both *bhikkhus* and laymen, had been inaugurated under the presidency of the Ven. Kirulapanē Vimala Mahā Nāyaka Thera, the Chief of the Kōṭṭe Chapter of the *Sangha* (*Kalyāṇi sāmagrī saṅgha sabhā*). This organization, considered to be purely national and cultural, had no political alliance with any party, and had declared that its aim was to make Sinhala the State language and to revive the national and cultural heritage. Many leading Buddhist monks and laymen were a part of this movement. It organized processions and festivals at Anurādhapura and Kataragama—highly respected ancient religious sites of popular pilgrimage—to awaken the national consciousness of the masses. Once, a procession of automobiles, beginning at the Śrī Laṅkā Vidyālaya (Buddhist temple) in Colombo, went along the southern coast to Tissamahārāma, the celebrated 2nd century B.C. Buddhist monastery in the south, then to Kataragama, the abode of the god Kataragama (Skanda), a powerful and popular deity, and returned to Colombo the following day through Ratnapura after paying homage there to another deity, Saman (Sumana) at the Maha Saman Dēvālaya. At some stages of this procession as many as 500 *bhikkhus* participated. Thousands of people, assembled to honor the procession, were exhorted to work for the revival of the national language and Buddhist culture. This movement enhanced the respect of the population for the *Sangha.* Only the Marxist parties, who stood at that time for parity for both Sinhala and Tamil languages, were opposed to this movement. (Today the attitude of these parties is quite different.) Finally, The *Sinhala Jātika Sangamaya* handed to the then Prime Minister, Sir John Kotalawala, a petition signed by one million people requesting the government to declare Sinhala the only state language in Ceylon. But nothing happened.

About the same period, under the leadership of the Ven. Hēnpiṭagedara Ñāṇasīha Thera, a learned and leading Buddhist monk, principal of a *pirivena,* and Mr. N. Q. Dias, a high-ranking civil servant, a campaign with a clearly defined aim of regaining the lost positions and privileges of Buddhists was launched. This, too, had no direct political affiliations. A series of societies, designated *Buddha Sāsana Samiti,* were established throughout the country to safeguard Buddhist interests.

Some time before the general election of 1956, another organization, *Eksat Bhikṣu Peramuṇa* (successor to the *Eksat Bhikṣu Maṇḍalaya*), composed exclusively of Buddhist monks, was born with the aim of advising and directing the people on political matters. (One of its leaders, the late Māpiṭigama Buddharakkhita Thera, incumbent of the Rāja Mahā Vihāra at Kälaṇiya near Colombo, one of the most celebrated and venerated Buddhist temples on the island, was later involved in the assassination of Prime Minister S. W. R. D. Bandaranaike, whom he himself had strongly supported in the 1956 general election.) This organization, one of the most prominent and influential at the time, held island-wide meetings urging people to support the party prepared to implement the proposals of the Buddhist Committee of Inquiry and to make Sinhala the only state language.

There was, generally speaking, a considerable agitation and awakening in the country for a revival of national language, culture, and religion, and for the recognition of the rights of the common man. Mr. S. W. R. D. Bandaranaike, a former cabinet minister of the United National Party (U.N.P.) government then in power, but at that time in the opposition and leader of the Śrī Laṅkā Freedom Party (S.L.F.P.), promised to implement those proposals if elected as head of the government.

Various organizations—the *Eksat Bhikṣu Peramuṇa* (United Front of *Bhikkhus* already mentioned), the *Bhāṣā Peramuṇa* (the Language Front, an organization of Sinhala teachers, writers, and poets including both *bhikkhus* and laymen, demanding Sinhala be made the State language), the *Āyurveda Saṅgamaya* (Congress of Indigenous Medical Practitioners)—all of whom had influence in rural districts, supported Mr. Bandaranaike. The United National Party, consisting of conservatives in the forefront of politics since 1931, was utterly defeated and Mr. Bandaranaike's S.L.F.P. came to power.

This was at the time hailed as a revolution, the victory of the common man. Certainly the common man, till then ignored and despised, except at election time, became conscious of his position in the country and consequently gained some self-respect and self-confidence. It was an important psychological change. National and Buddhist culture was given a more prominent place. Sinhala was declared the state language. Public transport and the handling of cargoes in the port of Colombo were nationalized. A Paddy Lands Bill offered the peasant cultivator some measure of security of tenure which he did not enjoy before. These indeed were some changes worthy of note after independence.

For the first time in Ceylon, Mr. Bandaranaike created a Ministry of Culture to be in charge of cultural and religious affairs. This also was a result of various Buddhist campaigns. Under the direction of this Ministry a series of societies called *Śāsanārakṣaka Samiti* (Societies for the Protection of the *Sāsana*) were created throughout the island; *daham pāsal,* schools for teaching Buddhism to children, were aided and supervised; campaigns were organized to interest and encourage young people in national art, literature, drama, sports, and public debating. This offered the opportunity for rural youth to emulate and compete with their more advanced urban counterparts.

National art with a long tradition, which was ignored during the colonial period, was revived. As early as 1948, Mañjuśrī Thera held an exhibition of his drawings in London and showed some magnificent copies of ancient mural paintings from Buddhist temples in Ceylon. Later, the Ven. Māpalagama Vipulasāra Thera, incumbent of the Parama Dhamma Chetiya temple, Director of Parama Dhamma Chetiya Pirivena and Pirivena Teachers' Training College at Ratmalana, a well-known artist and sculptor, popularized traditional art forms, decorations, and handicrafts. The National Arts Society of Ceylon, of which he is the founder-president, trains artists, sculptors, and artisans. *Lak-sala,* the popular store in Colombo Fort where traditional art objects and handicrafts of Ceylon are sold, was opened by the government to encourage national art, also at the instigation of Vipulasāra Thera. The Buddha statues made by this *bhikkhu* are venerated today not only in Ceylon, but also in India, Malaysia, Japan, England, Europe, and America.

From the Buddhist point of view, 1956 was highly important for another reason: it was the year of *Buddha Jayanti*, the 2500th anniversary of the Buddha. This was celebrated in all Buddhist countries in Asia and by Buddhist organizations in Europe and America. *Buddha Jayanti* celebrations generated a new impulse in Ceylon as well as in many other Buddhist countries. It was in fact after 1956 that the Buddhist and national revival in Ceylon (and in many other Buddhist countries) was revivified although it dates from a decade earlier. Scores of new books and journals appeared. The publication of the Pāli *Tipiṭaka* along with a Sinhala translation, the editing and publishing of an encyclopedia of Buddhism in English and of another encyclopedia in Sinhala were sponsored by the government. More schools to teach Buddhism to children (*daham pāsal*) were opened, mostly in Buddhist temples or temple premises. Religious classes and examinations began to be held even in prisons. Centers of meditation, both in urban and rural areas, increased and became popular. New Buddhist societies and organizations sprang up for various social and cultural purposes. Foreign street names used during the colonial period were replaced by Buddhist or national names. Large Buddha statues were installed in important public places and even on the premises of some government departments, almost as a visible sign of the re-assertion of lost Buddhist rights. State-aided centers for the training of *bhikkhus* were established. *Pirivenas* (monastic colleges) were classified as junior and senior, and their curricula were changed and improved to make them up to date. *Bhikkhus* took a more prominent and active part than earlier in the affairs of the country.

In line with this Buddhist reawakening, the prime minister, as he had promised during the elections, secured the passage of a resolution through Parliament to examine how to implement the recommendations set out in the Buddhist Committee's report. Accordingly, on March 4, 1957, the governor-general appointed a commission consisting of ten leading Buddhist monks and five laymen. Eight members of this body, known as the Buddha *Sāsana* Commission, even visited Burma, Thailand, Cambodia, and Laos to study Buddhist organizations and activities in those countries. On June 7, 1959, the commission submitted its report to the governor-general. Almost all the recommendations made by the Buddhist Committee of Inquiry in 1956 were approved by this commission, with some changes and modifications and suggestions on how to realize them.

The two most respected leading Buddhist monastic institutes, the Vidyodaya Pirivena and the Vidyālaṅkāra Pirivena, were granted full university status in 1959 by an Act of Parliament. According to this Act, the vice-chancellors of these two universities had to be Buddhist monks, following the old monastic college tradition. But they were open to both *bhikkhu* and lay students; only women were excluded. This was changed by another Act, in 1966: any qualified person, *bhikkhu* or layman, could be a vice-chancellor and women were admitted. Many *pirivenas* were affiliated with these two universities as their colleges. The aim of the creators of these two universities was, however, later unrealized and forgotten. Today they are no different from any other university in Ceylon or elsewhere.

In the universities young *bhikkhu* students, influenced by modern trends and ideas, became more independent and liberal than their Elders. Buddhist monks in Ceylon never go to movies and theaters as it is considered to be against their precepts. But the student monks in universities went to film shows and dramatic performances on the campus as a part of their education. This was deplored as improper by older people both of the *Sangha* and the laity who do not understand historical changes and developments which are inevitable.

However, more and more young *bhikkhus* received higher education and were increasingly engaged in educational and social activities. They were not content only with looking after their temples and performing religious rites and ceremonies. Some of them, for example, organized in rural areas *śrama-dāna* (gift of labor) groups, i.e., groups of people voluntarily helping the villagers by building their roads, digging their wells, erecting their houses, repairing their dilapidated old irrigation reservoirs, etc.

Bhikkhus who received appointments as teachers in schools were traditionally devoted to the instruction of children and improving schools. In some areas, parents of children were asking for Buddhist monks as principals of schools, because under their leadership they were better looked after. But there, too, was considerable criticism of these *bhikkhus*: as during the colonial period, there are people who are opposed to *bhikkhus* taking part in educational and welfare activities.

On September 25, 1959, Prime Minister S. W. R. D. Bandaranaike was assassinated. In this treacherous violence two Buddhist monks, among others, were involved. One of them was Māpiṭigama Budhharakkhita

Thera, one of the chief supporters and erstwhile intimate friends of the Prime Minister. The other was a visiting lecturer at the Āyurvedic (indigenous medicine) College in Colombo. The true story of this assassination still remains a mystery. Whatever it may be, it is generally believed that this crime was the result, not of any political differences, but of revenge and personal ambitions. The two *bhikkhus* and a layman were found guilty by the Supreme Court.

This tragic event was a severe set-back to *bhikkhus* in Ceylon. Although well-known elderly monks were respected and venerated and some were even invited to perform the funeral rites of the assassinated Prime Minister, generally speaking, *bhikkhus* could not face the public for several years.[2]

They appeared again on the political scene during the 1965 general election. This time a group of *bhikkhus,* who were earlier supporters of the S.L.F.P., worked for the U.N.P. because they were afraid that the Press Bill proposed by the S.L.F.P. coalition government would take away the freedom of expression and democratic rights of the people and that communism, if it came to power, would paralyze Buddhism in Ceylon as in China and Tibet. Mention should be made here of the *Trainikāyika Sangha Sabhā* (consisting of members of the *Sangha* of the three *nikāyas*), inaugurated in 1965 under the patronage of Mr. Hema Basnayaka, a former Chief Justice of Ceylon. One of the aims of this organization was to lead a campaign against the proposed Press Bill. In 1965 the S.L.F.P. was defeated and the U.N.P. came to power. Thus, *bhikkhus* on both sides were again in the forefront.

There are about one million members of the Buddhist *Sangha* in the world. Of these about 300,000 who belong to the Theravāda *Sangha* are in Bangla Desh, Burma, Cambodia, Ceylon, India, Laos, and Thailand while about 700,000 who are of the Mahāyāna *Sangha* live in China, Korea, Hawaii, Hong Kong, Japan, Malaysia, the Philippines, Singapore, and Vietnam. With the idea of bringing about understanding among them and drawing them closer together, and co-ordinating and harnessing their services for peace and the welfare of mankind, the World Buddhist *Sangha* Council was born in Ceylon on May 9, 1966, at the initiative of the Ven. Paṇḍita Piṁbure Sorata Thera, Principal of the Pirivena Teachers' Training College at the Parama Dhamma Chetiya monastery at Ratmalāna near Colombo. Inaugural sessions of this Council were held during five days and the Government of Ceylon gave every assistance. The *Sangha Rājas* (lit. "kings" of the *Sangha*) of Cambodia, Laos, and Thailand, invited by the Ceylon Government to attend this council, were treated as state guests. At the request of the Ven. Piṁbure Sorata Thera, Secretary-General of the World Buddhist *Sangha* Council, the author of this book presented to the Council held in Colombo on January 27, 1967, a formula consisting of nine basic points unifying the Theravāda and the Mahāyāna, which was unanimously accepted. (See Appendix IV)

The creation of Vidyodaya and Vidyālaṅkāra Universities, mentioned earlier, had far-reaching effects on the social and political life of Ceylon, more decisive than many people could ever have imagined. In order to understand this, even a very brief summary of the educational background of the country is necessary.

During the British period in Ceylon, as in all colonial countries, education was primarily designed to supply functionaries for the clerical and civil services necessary to run the government machine. It was not planned to produce men and women necessary for the real economic development of the country. Education in English, which opened the door to lucrative positions, was available only to a very limited circle, a privileged wealthy class, hardly five percent of the population, consisting of the elite. The balance of the population, poor peasants and working people, particularly those in remote rural areas, had great difficulty securing for their children even an elementary or secondary education in a "vernacular school" (if one was available). This "vernacular" education could not provide its recipients with anything economically worthwhile. A fairly good knowledge of English, a good working knowledge of it in fact, was absolutely necessary for reasonably paid employment. All "English schools" and colleges were in cities and towns, and they were very costly.

A University College, affiliated with London University, was established in Colombo in 1921 and became the autonomous University of Ceylon in 1942. Most students at this institution were the sons and daughters of the elite. The student of peasant and working-class parents was an exception.

In 1945, a free education plan was introduced. Many schools—elementary, secondary, and colleges—were opened even in predominantly rural areas. In most of these schools English was taught as a second language at an elementary level. Education up to and including university was free. Up to the age of 14 it was free and compulsory.

This education, disseminated widely throughout the island, raising its literacy to one of the highest in Asia, second only to that of Japan, differed little from that given during the colonial period. There were minor modifications, but no radical change. Thousands of students, qualified to receive a higher education, were unable to enter the existing University of Ceylon for two main reasons: (1) there was no room for them there; (2) in spite of the government policy of Sinhala as the national language and the reasonable use of Tamil, the language of instruction at the University of Ceylon was still English, and the vast majority of students from rural areas with little or no English could not fully comprehend their teachers.

A delegation met the Minister of Education in June 1956 and urged him to take immediate steps to enable these students fluent in Sinhala to obtain university degrees by the end of 1958. The minister consulted the vice-chancellor of Ceylon University, who advised that the most satisfactory solution would be the establishment of a second university. So, the Vidyodaya and Vidyālaṅkāra Pirivenas were given university status in 1959, and the door to higher education was opened to thousands of students from rural areas as well as to hundreds of young *bhikkhus*. Obviously, the medium of instruction in these two universities was Sinhala.

More than seventy-five percent of the students, including *bhikkhus,* who attended Vidyodaya and Vidyālaṅkāra Universities came from very poor peasant and working class backgrounds. But for these two institutions they never would have had an opportunity to receive any kind of higher education. Quite a few parents, with great hopes for the future, sold or mortgaged what little they had to educate their children. Some students were so poor that they spent the working day at the university without a meal. The government scheme of subsidies for poor students was inadequate. After all their privations, when these students left the university with their degrees or diplomas, all their hopes and the hopes of their elders collapsed; they could not find employment. Education in Ceylon was never, and still is not, planned to meet the manpower requirements for the development of the country. A vast majority of students received, and still receive, an education in liberal arts and languages. The high rate of graduate unemployment is therefore not surprising.

Since the early 1930's Marxist parties in Ceylon had been criticizing and condemning the prevailing political, economic, and social structure, and preaching "bloody" revolution. Many, particularly the younger generation, were attracted to this new movement. A majority of students, especially from poor families, attending high schools and universities, were admirers and followers of these revolutionary Marxist leaders, sincerely believing in their ability to solve their problems one day. In the universities, students who were members or supporters of the Śrī Laṅkā Freedom Party, which professes to be socialist, the Laṅkā Sama Samāja Party and the Communist Party, both known as Marxist, were elected by overwhelming majorities to offices of the student unions and councils.

Unemployment in Ceylon has been rising for several years. In the absence of reliable statistics, particularly for the rural areas, it is difficult to provide specific details. But it was estimated in 1970 that there were some 700,000 unemployed. Add to this about 12,000 unemployed university graduates, and it is easy to see why there was discontent. Only a small circle, the wealthy elite, was satisfied. The United National Party coalition which had been in power for five years since 1965 had signally failed to deal with the economic problems of the country.

In the general election of 1970, the S.L.F.P., L.S.S.P., and C.P.—the United Left Front—contested the election for the first time on a common election program. They promised to solve the problem of unemployment, promised to nationalize banks, plantations, big industries, etc., in short, to bring about revolutionary political, economic, and social changes intended to make Ceylon a truly socialist country. Thousands of students from high schools and universities, along with unemployed graduates, sincerely believing in the program and the propaganda of the United Left Front, went out into the country and worked hard, at personal risk to themselves, to put it into power. In addition, there were *bhikkhus,* school and university teachers, and various other forces united in their support for a socialist program.

In May 1970, the United Left Front swept into power with more than a two-thirds majority of seats in the House—unprecedented in the political history of Ceylon. The new government immediately recognized the governments of North Korea, North Vietnam, East Germany, and suspended diplomatic relations with Israel as a gesture of its socialist and revolutionary policy. But it seemed to be in no great hurry to implement any measures ameliorating the social and economic situation in the country.

The masses in rural and urban areas, suffering under inflation and unemployment, conscious of social and economic injustices, had always been complaining, humbly and timidly, about their hardships and difficulties. They were not educated; they had neither the knowledge nor the capacity to organize themselves effectively. Now their sons and daughters were educated; they understood the problems facing them; they had the knowledge, capacity, ability, and courage to organize themselves into a new revolutionary movement. The Marxist leaders, who had been preaching revolution, did not come from this class; they belonged to the wealthy elite. They were not even free from the conventional sense of values and the colonial mentality of the Ceylonese elite of the British period.[3] They kept talking about the suffering of the masses, but they themselves were in a very different class. They were as wealthy as any wealthy people in Ceylon. Their revolutionary slogans were political cliches useful during election campaigns. A revolution now would not have been in their interest—they had nothing to gain and everything to lose. On the other hand, these young people who had put them in power were the sons and daughters of peasants, workers, and the humblest of the petite bourgeoisie. They had nothing to lose by a revolution, but everything to gain. Here was the basic and fundamental difference between the government and the most formidable section of its supporters.

About seven or eight months after the 1970 general elections these young people's political groups, organized earlier under the name of the Janatā Vimukti Peramuṇa (People's Liberation Front), held mass meetings in Colombo and in provincial towns declaring that they had, with one hand, helped this government which called itself socialist to come to power, and that they were ready, with both hands, to support it to advance toward socialism. They severely criticized it, however, particularly its Marxist leaders, for failing to fulfill their election promises. J.V.P. meetings became very popular and attracted enormous crowds. They indicated that if the government did not implement their promised socialist program, there could be a revolutionary action. As was to be expected, a number of *bhikkhus* were associated with this movement.

The government lacked the wisdom or courage to meet these young people in a frank discussion of the situation; if they had, it might perhaps have produced some satisfactory results. Instead, they began by harassing and imprisoning the leaders of the J.V.P. They then proclaimed a state of emergency in March 1971 and banned the J.V.P. A strict censorship was enforced. In desperation, the young revolutionaries, from April 5, 1971, began a series of uncoordinated attacks on police stations and took control of some rural districts. The government panicked. Marxist leaders, who had been preaching revolution for the last 35 years, were overtaken by their own creation. The youthful revolutionary movement was so courageous and disciplined that in the first few weeks the army and the police found it difficult to cope with it. The prime minister immediately appealed to various foreign countries for help. England, the United States, the Soviet Union, Yugoslavia, the United Arab Republic, India, and Pakistan immediately provided arms and ammunitions. The People's Republic of China made a very large loan to the Government of Ceylon and categorically supported it in its campaign.

Emergency regulations passed in March 1971 by the government opened the door to police and military terrorism. These regulations permitted the arrest of persons without warrant, their detention without trial, and the burial or cremation of dead bodies by police officers or members of the armed service without inquest or compliance with the provisions of any other written law. The police and the army were given unlimited powers, and the country was governed by terror. Thousands of young men and women were arrested, tortured, mutilated, shot, and even burned alive. Dead bodies, some decapitated, floated down the rivers. Girls were stripped naked, raped, tortured, and killed. Hundreds of *bhikkhus,* mostly from the Vidyodaya and Vidyālaṅkāra Universities, were arrested, humiliated, tortured, or killed. Atrocities and cruelties of such magnitude had been unheard of since the time of the Portuguese in the 16th century.[4] Public opinion puts the number killed at about 10,000. Some believe it might run to anything between 15,000 and 20,000. The prime minister declared that no more than 1,200 were actually killed in skirmishes with the police and the army.

Between 14,000 and 16,000 were arrested and imprisoned. Vidyodaya and Vidyālaṅkāra Universities were converted to prison camps under the euphemistic designation of "rehabilitation centers." It is from these two universities that many of the young revolutionaries and some of their leaders came. It was an ironic symbol that these same universities became their prisons.

However one judges these young men and women, their courage of conviction, determination, sacrifice, discipline, honesty of purpose and character are qualities of which any nation in the world would be proud. They are the lost generation of our country, betrayed by those in whom they put their trust. If these young people were misguided, as the government chooses to put it, what of those who led them astray by their precepts and their preaching?

The government is reported to be afraid to recruit young men under 35 years for the police or the armed forces in a country where seventy percent of the population is under 35. Under the emergency regulations, the civil rights and liberties of the people were suppressed. This crisis in Ceylon, a country reputedly democratic, led to the birth of a Civil Rights Movement headed by university dons, lawyers, doctors, Buddhist monks, Catholic and Protestant clergy, artists, writers, and various intellectuals. An international committee in London has been formed for the purpose of arousing world opinion about the situation prevailing in Ceylon.

Meanwhile, a new constitution was adopted and Ceylon was declared, on May 22, 1972, the Republic of Śrī Laṅkā. (Laṅkā or Śrī Laṅkā is not a new name as many people in foreign countries suppose. It was the name used in ancient chronicles, inscriptions, and literature, and it is the name always used by the people of the country. "Ceylon" was and is used only in foreign languages.) Under the new constitution Buddhism occupies the primary place and Sinhala becomes the official language.

The United Left Front Government, which began to ignore and neglect *bhikkhus* after the 1970 general election, became almost hostile to them since the insurgency in 1971. There is a covert move on the part of the government, under the pretext of protecting Buddhism, to restrict the activities of *bhikkhus* and to deny them some civil rights which are common to all citizens. There are four recognized religions in Ceylon: Buddhism, Hinduism, Christianity, and Islam. To make laws and regulations discriminating against the clergy of one religion is absolutely contrary to all democratic principles. This move is already being opposed not only by Buddhist monks, but also by non-Buddhists, as a flagrant violation of human rights.

The events of the last few decades show that the *bhikkhu* tradition of being socially conscious and active in the life of the country has remained, and that in spite of suppressive measures, *bhikkhus* continue to maintain that tradition, in accordance with the advice of the Buddha, "for the welfare of the many, for the happiness of the many, out of compassion for the world"—*bahujanahitāya, bahujanasukhāya, lokānukampāya.*

APPENDIX I

WHAT IS POLITICS?

The idea that *bhikkhus* should not participate in political activities has of late circulated among some people in Ceylon. Lack of understanding and respect for politics is one of the causes for this attitude. It is indeed sad to note that not only ordinary citizens but also some of the Ministers of State and Members of Parliament do not seem to have a true understanding of the meaning of politics. There has been no period in the history of this country when its ignorance of the meaning of politics is as well demonstrated as today.

The English word "politics" as well as the Sinhala word *deśapālana,* in their usage have gone beyond their original etymological sense and have embraced a vast scope. Today, a dictionary definition is insufficient. Its contemporary connotation is extensive. Politics is a highly developed science with different branches and ramifications.

Several articles recently published in newspapers show that to some politics is a base, mean, low enterprise not to be touched by noble-minded, virtuous, and pious people of good character; it is an occupation of dishonest, crafty, and cunning people.[1]

John Wilkes, a contemporary of Dr. Johnson (1709–1784 A.C.), published an obscene article about women in the newspaper *North Briton*. He was disgraced; the law punished him, and he went to jail. Nevertheless,

John Wilkes, who preached patriotism and conducted his political campaigns on patriotic and nationalist sentiment, was on five occasions elected a Member of Parliament. Dr. Johnson, who was famous for his sarcasm and irony, once said, in talking about John Wilkes: "Patriotism is the last refuge of a scoundrel." This was hardly a true exposition of patriotism. It was only sarcasm at the expense of a particular character.

Similarly, it may be that certain people of this country speak of politics as "the last refuge of scoundrels," because they have become disillusioned with the character and activities of some of those who have taken to politics: activities such as tempting voters with liquor, bribery, thuggery with the aid of hoodlums to harass innocent voters during election times; and once in Parliament, bribery, nepotism, and irresponsible behavior. All this has no doubt led to politics being considered as "the last refuge of scoundrels." Similarly, many people write and speak of a thing called "the political arena" because of fights, quarrels, and brawls during election campaigns. According to the opinion of a certain *nāyaka thera,* politics is "thieving" or "fraud."[2]

But this opprobrium built into the word "politics" does not arise out of anything intrinsically ignominious in politics itself, but is produced by the viciousness of those who have taken to politics.

The ordinary man in the street thinks of "politics" as a couple of intoxicating drinks and selling his vote for a few rupees. From the utterances made by some *nāyaka theras,* the editors of some newspapers, and some Members of Parliament, it appears that politics is nothing more than contesting a seat in the Parliament and winning it. Such childishness has not been heard of except in the recent past. It is certainly no secret that the political services rendered by men with such ideas are limited only to winning a seat in the Parliament.

A declaration by the *mahā nāyaka thera* of the Malvatta Chapter says that the first, second, and third stages in Ceylonese politics should be the village committees, urban and municipal councils, and the Parliament respectively.[3] Bernard Shaw remarked however: "But parliaments and municipalities do not cover the whole political field."[4]

Mahatma Gandhi is well known the world over as a great political figure and a statesman. Yet he never contested a seat in any legislature. All he did was directed towards winning the freedom of India and improving the lot of his countrymen. For this he toiled day and night at great personal sacrifice. But of course, according to the opinion of our political pundits, Gandhiji cannot be considered a politician.

According to Buddhism, politics is noble service for the well being of others to be rendered in accordance with the "Ten Duties of the King."[5] One who takes to politics should be endowed with the "Four Qualities of Benevolence."[6] According to Buddhism, politics is a righteous deed. The customary stanza sung by the Buddhist monks at the end of religious ceremonies or functions embodies economic, social, and political aspirations.[7]

Politics is connected with life. So is religion. The two can never be separated. What the mind is to the body, religion is to politics. Politics bereft of religion becomes sin and evil. What is meant by religion here is not external rites and ceremonies of established or institutionalized religion, but the development of moral and spiritual character through the cultivation of such qualities as love, compassion, and wisdom. Political administration undertaken by those who, lacking such sublime thoughts and virtuous qualities, have no character, can only spell disaster instead of prosperity to the world.

Guided by Buddhist principles and ideas, Emperor Asoka of India built a righteous empire in the 3rd century B.C. The *Mahāvaṃsa* shows that from time to time similar kingdoms were established in Ceylon, too.

The *Manusmṛti* says that the duty of a king ruling a country is to protect his people, not to oppress them.[8]

It is needless recounting here that in his writings and speeches Mahatma Gandhi always emphasized that politics should not be separated from virtue, morality, and righteousness; that it should be deemed a noble religious duty and practiced as such; that it should be cleansed of those hypocritical, self-seekers of evil character who dominate it at present and that it should be the work of virtuous and magnanimous people. He says that he took to politics because of his devotion to religion. He declares that those who cry for the separation of religion from politics are ignorant not only of religion but also of politics. The poet, William Blake, queries: "Are not politics and religion the same things?"

Twenty-three centuries ago, Aristotle said: "Man is by nature a political animal."[9]

A conscientious person, who understands right and wrong, who has a sense of responsibility, and who lives in an organized society cannot live without participating in politics: education, the conduct of life, the suppression of crimes, morality, health and sanitation, agriculture and industry, rural development, food, clothing, housing, communications, trade, commerce, and a hundred other problems, big and small, connected with human society, are all included in politics.

"On all sides men are agreed that problems of poverty, problems of education, problems of physical, mental, and moral efficiency are matters not merely [for the] individual . . . but equally [are] of public and governmental concern," said Dr. Hobhouse, Professor of Sociology at the University of London.[10] It is the function of politics to resolve these problems justly and equitably in such a manner as would be most beneficial to the greatest number.

"Politics is the study of the relations existing between individuals and between groups," says Delisle Burns.[11] Explaining the same idea in a different way he states: "In the most general sense politics is concerned with the relation of man to man in civilized society."[12]

The following from Bernard Shaw makes it very clear that politics is purely a science of social life: "They think of politics as something outside life, though politics are either the science of social life or nothing."[13]

Harold Laski, Professor of Political Science at the University of London, says: "The State is thus a way of regulating human conduct."[14]

Aristotle says that the aim of politics is to render the highest good to the greatest number:

> Every state is a community of some kind, and every community is established with a view to some good; for mankind always acts in order to obtain that which they think good. But, if all communities aim at some good, the state or political community which is the highest of all, and which embraces all the rest, aims at good in a greater degree than any other, and at the highest good.[15]

Once again, according to Laski: "The State is thus a fellowship of men aiming at the enrichment of the common life."[16] The difference between this society and other societies lies in the fact that those who live within it must necessarily and obligatorily join in enriching the common life; what is expected of its members could be obtained even by compulsion. Laski further says: "It is judged by what it offers to its members in terms of the things they deem to be good. Its roots are laid in their minds and hearts."[17]

Delisle Burns says that ". . . the interest of the political thinker is the maintenance and development of civilized life . . . political facts are those which are involved in the betterment of human life, called the progress of civilization, material, intellectual, and emotional."[18]

From these various expositions of authorities in the field of political science, and also from the opinions of wise men of the past, it is plain that politics is not a "fraud," not an "arena," not "the last refuge of the scoundrel." On the contrary, it is a noble service for the good and well being of the world, a pursuit to be undertaken by pious, virtuous, and honest people of noble and exemplary character. In short, politics constitutes the development of such things as education, morality, health, sanitation, social and economic security, all of which are necessary and conducive to the good and well being of mankind both here and hereafter.

Now it is interesting to examine why some consider it unworthy of *bhikkhus* to engage in such noble and exalted service which is for the good and well being of humanity.

One reason for this attitude is the misunderstanding

of politics and of Buddhism and the *bhikkhu*-life. Some people are of the opinion that *bhikkhus* need not participate in any activity intended for the progress and well being of the people and that they should live away from society, enjoying the requisites provided by the people, unmindful of what is happening to people, and intent only on their salvation—an utterly selfish and egoistic life! This is indeed a gross misconception and misunderstanding of Buddhism and the *bhikkhu's* life. It loses sight entirely of the noble and lofty ideals and teachings of Buddhism.

The *bhikkhu* is not a selfish, cowardly individual thinking only of his happiness and salvation, unmindful of whatever happens to the rest of humanity. A true *bhikkhu* is an altruistic, heroic person who considers others' happiness more than his own. He, like the Bodhisattva Sumedha, will renounce his own *nirvāṇa* for the sake of others. Buddhism is built upon service to others. One who is concerned only with one's own happiness and salvation, unmindful of whatever happens to others, cannot be considered even to be an ordinary Buddhist, leave alone a Buddhist monk.

If a pious and virtuous *bhikkhu,* whose mind is developed and purified through meditation, with no selfish motives, works for the good and happiness of people here and hereafter—whether this is labelled politics or not—is it not erroneous and un-Buddhistic to believe that his work is contrary to Buddhism or that it is improper for a *bhikkhu?* Surely there is no nobler life than this in the world.

Some people fear that political activities or social work will interfere with the piety of a *bhikkhu.* Yet, a *bhikkhu* who is bereft of virtue, whose mind and character are not developed through meditation, can never render any real service to the people. If anyone thinks that this is possible, it surely is a supreme deception. A *bhikkhu* engaged in social work must necessarily possess nobler and more exalted virtues and qualities than a *bhikkhu* living by himself and meditating in retirement in a forest. But just as there are *bhikkhus* who are not pure in mind and character among the forest-dwelling monks, it is certain that there are *bhikkhus* impure in mind and character among the monks participating in social and welfare activities.

It is unthinkable that the present-day *bhikkhu* population of over 15,000[19] will, all of them, retire to the forest for meditation. Are they all to continue to live this meaningless and lazy life both in respect of themselves and of others, which is just another burden to the country and the nation? Or should they occupy themselves in a course of action that will be of use to themselves, to the country, to the nation, and to the religion?

This is not merely a religious question. This is a very grave question of religious, national, economic, and social import.

Another group of people who disapprove of *bhikkhus* participating in political activities is that wealthy, powerful, and aristocratic coterie which has inequitably usurped political as well as other powers and privileges in the country. They fear that once the *bhikkhus* become active in political issues their unjust treatment of the poor might be publicly exposed, to the detriment of the power they enjoy. This fear, of course, is legitimate.[20]

It is a well-known fact that in the recent past many high priests (*nāyaka theras*) and chief monks of temples belonging to several sects openly supported and campaigned in favor of certain candidates in the past general elections. Everybody accepted this as political work. No conferences were held to dissuade them from such activities. Nor was public opinion aroused against them through banner headlines and articles in the newspapers. Nevertheless, a certain group of people is today campaigning against *bhikkhus* participating in politics. What is the reason for this?

In those days high priests and other *bhikkhus* participated in political activities neither with a conviction of the meaning of politics nor in accordance with any political principles, but merely at the request of wealthy and influential aristocratic leaders. It was simply surrender and subordination to the wealthy and the powerful. But today the situation is different. *Bhikkhus* who have acquired a good modern education have an insight into current problems, and through their devotion to their country, their nation, and their religion, have come forward freely and independently to tell the masses of their legitimate rights and privileges, without subordinating themselves to the will of the powerful and wealthy aristocrats. These who have unjustly appropriated to themselves the power in the country are too well aware of the danger to which they are being exposed by the course of action taken by these *bhikkhus*. As a measure of self-preservation, therefore, as far as they are concerned, *bhikkhus* must be excluded from political activities.

Even though rural reconstruction and development come within the purview of politics, the wealthy and powerful have not so far objected to *bhikkhus* participating in such activities. The reason for this is that until now rural reconstruction and development plans have been carried out according to the ideas and the advice of the rich and government officials. The result has been that the interests of the rich have been safeguarded and the legitimate rights and privileges of the poor have not been granted to them. What has actually happened is that helpless villagers have been frightened and humbled; they have been trained to subordinate themselves to the rich and to officialdom. This is, in fact, an impediment to national development and national freedom.

It can certainly be divined today that if, at some time in the future, *bhikkhus* embark on a genuine program of rural reconstruction to safeguard the legitimate rights and privileges of the destitute villagers and liberate them from the clutches of those powerful, rich landlords who keep them suppressed, if *bhikkhus* do reveal the truth and expose the corruptions of those who wield power today and tell the poor villagers that the rich have been responsible for the wretchedness in which they live, then on that day there will begin conferences and newspaper propaganda to declare that rural reconstruction and development work is improper for *bhikkhus* and that it will be disastrous for religion!

Some of our wealthy Buddhist leaders object not only to the *bhikkhus* participating in what they imagine to be politics, but also to the *bhikkhus* engaging themselves in educational and other important activities. Though the latter objection is scarcely voiced, it is obvious.[21]

The Buddhist Theosophical Society is a Buddhist association engaged in promoting Buddhist education. It was started by Colonel H. S. Olcott with the assistance of Buddhist monks. But today *bhikkhus* have no position in it. *Bhikkhus* do not have even the right to membership in this association. All positions of authority and office in it are held by rich laymen. The Ceylon Buddhist Congress is not a political party. It is an association which deals with the development of Buddhism. There, too, all key positions are held by the laymen. *Bhikkhus* have no place in it. The situation with numerous other societies and associations is hardly different.[22]

One of the reasons for this is the unfounded fear in the minds of wealthy Buddhist leaders that if intelligent, educated, and able *bhikkhus* do become active in these areas, their own position will be jeopardized. But the *bhikkhus* are not competing with them; they want only to render service to their country. It would be unfortunate if the *bhikkhu* is obstructed in order to maintain and safeguard vested interests.

APPENDIX II

BHIKKHUS AND POLITICS

Declaration of the Vidyālaṅkāra Pirivena
Passed unanimously on February 13, 1946

The Buddha permitted *bhikkhus* to change minor rules of the *Vinaya* if they so desire. Nevertheless, there is no historical evidence to show that the *bhikkhus* of the Theravāda school have on any occasion actually changed the rules of the *Vinaya.* Likewise, we do not say that even now they should be changed.

But it has to be admitted that the political, economic, and social conditions of today are different from those of the time of the Buddha, and that consequently the life of *bhikkhus* today is also different from that of the *bhikkhus* at that time.

In those days the ideal of monks generally was to realize *nirvāna* in their very lifetime. In later times their ideal was to exert themselves to the best of their ability in activities beneficial to themselves and others with a view to realizing *nirvāna* in a future life.

It is clearly seen that as a result of this very change, a great many other changes not known in the earlier days took place in the life of *bhikkhus* in later times.

The extent to which the life of monks today has undergone change can be clearly gauged when we take into consideration the prevailing conditions of life in temples, monasteries, and *pirivenas,* the teaching and learning of Sinhala, Sanskrit and such other subjects, the present system of examinations, the editing and writing of books and journals, conferring and accepting nāyakaships and such other titles, participation in various societies and being elected as officers in them. It has to be accepted, therefore, that, although the rules of the *Vinaya* have remained unaltered, the life of monks has undergone change and that this change is inevitable.

We believe that politics today embraces all fields of human activity directed towards the public weal. No one will dispute that the work for the promotion of the religion is the duty of the *bhikkhu.* It is clear that the welfare of the religion depends on the welfare of the people who profess that religion. History bears evidence to the fact that whenever the Sinhala nation—which was essentially a Buddhist nation—was prosperous, Buddhism also flourished. We, therefore, declare that it is nothing but fitting for *bhikkhus* to identify themselves with activities conducive to the welfare of our people—whether these activities be labelled politics or not—as long as they do not constitute an impediment to the religious life of a *bhikkhu.*

We cannot forget that from the earliest days the Sinhala monks, while leading the lives of *bhikkhus,* were in the forefront of movements for the progress of their nation, their country, and their religion.

Even today *bhikkhus* by being engaged actively in education, rural reconstruction, anti-crime campaigns, relief work, temperance work, social work and such other activities, are taking part in politics, whether they are aware of it or not. We do not believe that it is wrong for *bhikkhus* to participate in these activities.

We believe that it is incumbent on the *bhikkhu* not only to further the efforts directed towards the welfare of the country, but also to oppose such measures as are detrimental to the common good. For example, if any effort is made to obstruct the system of free education, the great boon which has been recently conferred on our people, it is the paramount duty of the *bhikkhu* not only to oppose all such efforts but also to endeavor to make it a permanent blessing.

In ancient days, according to the records of history, the welfare of the nation and the welfare of the religion were regarded as synonymous terms by the laity as well as by the *Sangha.* The divorce of religion from the nation was an idea introduced into the minds of the Sinhalese by invaders from the West, who belonged to an alien faith. It was a convenient instrument of astute policy to enable them to keep the people in subjugation in order to rule the country as they pleased. It was in their own interests, and not for the welfare of the people, that these foreign invaders attempted to create a gulf between the *bhikkhus* and the laity—a policy which they implemented with diplomatic cunning. We should not follow their example, and should not attempt to withdraw *bhikkhus* from society. Such conduct would assuredly be a deplorable act of injustice, committed against our nation, our country, and our religion.

Therefore, we publicly state that both our *bhikkhus* and our Buddhist leaders should avoid the pitfall of acting hastily, without deliberation and foresight, and should beware of doing a great disservice to our nation and to our religion.

K. Paññāsāra

Principal, Vidyālaṅkara Pirivena,
Tipiṭaka-Vāgīśvarācārya Upādhyāya,
Chief High Priest of the Colombo
and Chilaw Districts

February 2, 1946, Vidyālaṅkāra Pirivena

APPENDIX III

THE KĀLAṆIYA DECLARATION OF INDEPENDENCE

January 6, 1947

Hail

The Declaration of the *Sangha* of Śrī Laṅkā

Twenty-five centuries ago, our forefathers established in Śrī Laṅkā a state of Society, Free, Independent and Sovereign, in order to ensure to the people security of Life and Liberty on the one hand, and on the other the right as well as opportunity to seek and obtain Happiness. A few centuries later, the *Sangha,* the Treasurers of the eternal values proclaimed by the Buddha, became the Guardians of the Life and Liberty as well as the Sponsors of the Well-being and Happiness of that Society.

Nations and civilizations are not eternal. They rise, flourish, decay, and die. Nothing in this world can be regarded as eternal. There are values higher than cities and nations, and our country has always stood for these values. More material possessions are not the *sine qua non* of happiness. No measures or quantities of these can give that essential quality of happiness which constitutes the real dignity of mankind.

Four and a half centuries ago, "disturbers of the peace of mankind" from the West not only challenged the right of the people of this Island to their way of life and liberty, but also attempted to introduce into it ideals other than those which this country had always stood for. It is our glory that the country never had any dearth of men inspired with the spirit of Śrī Laṅkā. These outstanding leaders of the nation accepted the challenge, and fierce struggles by the people against the foreigners ensued during three whole centuries.

Thereafter a section of the community, abrogating to themselves an authority that had not the sanction of the will of the nation, ceded the country to the last of the alien aggressors, who have since dominated over it to the loss of liberty and happiness of its people. Posterity, however, cannot be deprived of the inherent rights which people acquire when they form themselves into a state of civilized society, by the act or acts, or Compact, or Convention entered into by any group of men in the near or remote past. And the people, who for one hundred and thirty-one years have been denied their inherent rights, are not content, today, to be fettered any longer or to remain under an alien yoke.

We, therefore, the *Saṅgha* of Śrī Laṅkā, the Guardians of the Life and Liberty and Sponsors of the Well-being and Happiness of the people of this Island, assembled on this hallowed spot sanctified by the touch of the feet of the Master, do hereby declare and publish, on behalf of the people, that Śrī Laṅkā claims its right to be a Free and Independent Sovereign State, that it has resolved to absolve itself from all allegiance to any other Power, State, or Crown, and that all political connection between it and any other State, is hereby dissolved; and that as a Free and Independent Sovereign State it has full right to safeguard its Freedom and Independence, to contract alliances and do all other acts and things which Independent States may of right do.

For due recognition of the rectitude of our action and for support of the claim made under this Declaration, we, the *Saṅgha* of Śrī Laṅkā, hereby appeal to the conscience and sense of justice of all right-thinking peoples of the world. And in hereby calling upon the good people of Śrī Laṅkā, on whose behalf we make this Declaration, unitedly and in courage and strong endeavor to see to it that its purpose is achieved in the fullest possible measure, we, the *Saṅgha* of Śrī Laṅka, on our part, pledge ourselves to associate with them in spirit as well as in action in that great and high resolve.

Declared on this auspicious anniversary of the Buddha's first visit to Śrī Laṅkā, Monday, the full-moon day of Durutu, in the year 2490 of the Buddhist era in the new *Gandhakuṭi* [Fragrant Chamber] of the Śrī Kalyāṇi Rāja Mahā Vihāra.

APPENDIX IV

BASIC POINTS UNIFYING THE THERAVĀDA AND THE MAHĀYĀNA

presented on January 27, 1967 to
The World Buddhist *Sangha* Council
by
The Ven. Dr. Walpola Śrī Rāhula
Tripiṭakavāgīśvarācārya
Vice-Chancellor, Vidyodaya University of Ceylon

1 The Buddha is our only Master.

2 We take refuge in the Buddha, the *Dhamma* and the *Sangha.*

3 We do not believe that this world is created and ruled by a god.

4 Following the example of the Buddha, who is the embodiment of Great Compassion (*mahā-karuṇā*) and Great Wisdom (*mahā-prajñā*), we consider that the purpose of life is to develop compassion for all living beings without discrimination and to work for their good, happiness, and peace; and to develop wisdom leading to the realization of Ultimate Truth.

5 We accept the Four Noble Truths, namely *Dukkha,* the Arising of *Dukkha,* the Cessation of *Dukkha,* and the Path leading to the Cessation of *Dukkha;* and the universal law of cause and effect as taught in the *pratītya-samutpāda* (Conditioned Genesis or Dependent Origination).

6 We understand, according to the teaching of the

Buddha, that all conditioned things (*saṃskāra*) are impermanent (*anitya*) and *dukkha,* and that all conditioned and unconditioned things (*dharma*) are without self (*anātma*).

7 We accept the Thirty-seven Qualities conducive to Enlightenment (*bodhipakṣa-dharma*) as different aspects of the Path taught by the Buddha leading to Enlightenment.

8 There are three ways of attaining *bodhi* or Enlightenment, according to the ability and capacity of each individual: namely as a disciple (*śrāvaka*), as a Pratyeka-Buddha and as a Samyak-sam-Buddha (Perfectly and Fully Enlightened Buddha). We accept it as the highest, noblest, and most heroic to follow the career of a Bodhisattva and to become a Samyak-sam-Buddha in order to save others.

9 We admit that in different countries there are differences with regard to the life of Buddhist monks, popular Buddhist beliefs and practices, rites and ceremonies, customs and habits. These external forms and expressions should not be confused with the essential teachings of the Buddha.

GLOSSARY OF TERMS

(Most of the terms used in this book are taken from Pāli Scriptures which constitute the earliest extant Buddhist Canon.)

Abhidhamma "super-doctrine," "higher doctrine," dealing with Buddhist philosophy and psychology.

Abhidhamma-piṭaka "The Canon of the Super-doctrine or Higher Doctrine." The group of 7 canonical books containing philosophical and psychological doctrines.

Ajjava honesty, integrity.

Akkodha freedom from hatred.

Alu-vihāra the ancient rock-temple at Mātalē in Central Ceylon where, in the 1st century B.C., the Pāli *Tipiṭaka* (*q.v.*) was for the first time committed to writing.

Anaṇa-sukha happiness of freedom from financial debt.

Anatta No-Soul, No-Self.

Anavajja-sukha happiness of leading a blameless life.

Aṅguttara-nikāya "The Book of the Gradual Sayings," the Collection containing the sayings of the Buddha arranged in numerical order. This *Nikāya* (*q.v.*) belongs to the *Sutta-piṭaka* (*q.v.*).

Anicca impermanent; impermanence.

Aniccā vata saṃkhārā "All conditioned things are indeed impermanent." The first line of a verse which is usually recited at funeral ceremonies. This verse was also recited by Sakka, king of gods, when the Buddha passed away.

Arahant one who is free from all fetters, defilements and impurities, and who is emancipated and perfect through the realization of *nirvāṇa* in the final stage, and who is free from rebirth.

Ārakkha-sampadā success in saving and protecting one's income and wealth.

Araṇya-vāsī "forest-dweller," a monk living in a forest. Cf. *Grāma-vāsī.*

Asiggāhaka "Sword-bearer," a high office, a royal honor conferred on very important personages. (For details see *History of Buddhism in Ceylon* by Walpola Rāhula, Gunasena & Co., Colombo, pp. xxxix, 74, 101, 104.)

Atthacariyā benevolent, useful conduct.

Atthisukha happiness of wealth, happiness of economic security.

Avihiṃsā (*Ahiṃsā*) non-violence.

Avirodha non-opposition, non-obstruction.

Bahujana-hitāya "for the good of the many."

Bahujana-sukhāya "for the happiness of the many."

Bhikkhu lit. "a mendicant monk," a Buddhist monk, *i.e.,* a person ordained into the Order of the *Sangha* (*q.v.*).

Bhoga-sukha happiness of enjoying one's wealth by spending it intelligently.

Bodhisattva a person who, out of great compassion for the world to save others, decides, aspires and perfects himself and finally becomes a Perfect and Fully Enlightened Buddha—*Arhat Samyaksambuddha.*

Brahmin a member of the highest caste, Brāhmaṇa caste, in India.

Cakkavattisīhanāda-sutta Discourse No. 26 of the *Dīgha-nikāya* (*q.v.*), dealing with such subjects as war, wickedness, wealth, poverty, crime, immorality.

Cullavagga one of the five books of the *Vinaya-piṭaka* (*q.v.*).

Dāgäba a Sinhala word derived from Pāli *dhātu-gabbha* (Skt. *dhātu-garbha*), which lit. means "chamber of relics," now commonly used, particularly in Ceylon, as an equivalent of *stūpa* or *cetiya* (Skt. *caitya*). A *dāgäba* supposedly enshrines the bodily relics of the Buddha or at least the bodily relics of a disciple who was *arahant* (*q.v.*).

Dāna charity, giving for another's benefit.

Deśapālana lit. "governing the country," politics.

Dhamma (Skt. *Dharma*) Truth, Teaching, Doctrine, righteousness, piety, morality, justice, nature, etc.; all conditioned and unconditioned things and states.

Dhamma-kathika "preacher of the doctrine."

Dhammapada one of the best known Buddhist canonical texts, containing 423 Pāli verses divided into 26 chapters.

Dhammapadaṭṭhakathā the Commentary on the *Dhammapada*.

Dīgha-nikāya "The Collection of Long Discourses." One of the five Collections containing the teachings of the Buddha. This *nikāya* (*q.v.*) belongs to the *Sutta-piṭaka* (*q.v.*).

Dīpavaṃsa "The Chronicle of the Island," a history of Ceylon written in Pāli verse about the 4th century A.C.

Dukkha lit. "suffering," but as the first of the four Noble Truths further denotes conflict, unsatisfactoriness, unsubstantiality, emptiness.

Gandha-kuṭi lit. "Fragrant Chamber." The word used for the room occupied by the Buddha. Today it is used even for the inner sanctuary housing the Buddha-image.

Gantha-dhura lit. "Occupation or duty or responsibility of books," *i.e.*, scholarship, learning, study, term used to denote the duty of a Buddhist monk with regard to scholarship, learning and teaching.

Grāma-vāsī lit. "village-dweller," "dwelling in the village," term used to denote monks living in villages and towns. (Cf. *araṇya-vāsī.*)

Kachcheri administrative headquarters of a district.

Kalyāṇamittatā good friendship, having a good friend who leads you along the right path.

Kammaṭṭhāna a topic of meditation.

Kandyan Convention an agreement signed by the British and the Sinhalese when the authority of the Sinhala kingdom was transferred to the British Government on March 2, 1815, in Kandy, the last capital of the Sinhala kings.

Karuṇā compassion.

Katikāvat covenant of the *Sangha* (*q.v.*).

Khanti patience, forebearance, tolerance.

Khuddānukhuddaka-sikkhāpada lesser and minor precepts.

Kūṭadanta-sutta Discourse No. 5 of the *Dīgha-nikāya* (*q.v.*).

Lābha-sīmā "Income area," the boundaries of landed property donated to a Buddhist monastery.

Lokānukampāya "out of compassion for the world."

Maddava gentleness, softness.

Mahā Thera great elder.

Mahāvagga one of the 5 books of the *Vinaya-piṭaka* (*q.v.*).

Mahāvaṃsa "The Great Chronicle," the history of Ceylon written in Pāli verse in the 5th century A.C., and continued by several successive authors up to the present century.

Mahā-vihāra the Great Monastery established in Anurādhapura in Ceylon in the 3rd century B.C., which became the center of the orthodox Theravāda (*q.v.*) tradition that spread later to other countries in Southeast Asia. The great Commentator Buddhaghosa (5th century A.C.), residing at this monastery, following the Mahāvihāra tradition, wrote his celebrated *Visuddhimagga* and translated into Pāli (*q.v.*) all major Sinhala commentaries on the *Tipiṭaka* (*q.v.*). The *Dīpavaṃsa* (*q.v.*) and the *Mahāvaṃsa* (*q.v.*) were composed also at this monastery. It was a Buddhist "university" like Nālandā in India, and students from foreign lands went to Anurādhapura to study at the Mahāvihāra there. (See Appendix I, "What was the Mahāvihāra" in *History of Buddhism in Ceylon* by Walpola Rāhula, Gunasena & Co., Colombo, p. 303.)

Mahāyāna "Great Vehicle," form of Buddhism prevalent in China, Japan, Korea, Mongolia, Tibet, Nepal, Vietnam, some regions of India.

Majjhima-nikāya "The Middle Length Sayings," one of the five Collections containing the discourses and sayings of the Buddha. This *nikāya* belongs to the *Sutta-piṭaka* (*q.v.*).

Manusmṛti "The Law of Manu," the book containing the Hindu social and moral law.

Mihintalē a hill near Anurādhapura where Buddhism was introduced to Ceylon by Mahinda, son of Asoka (Emperor of India), in the 3rd century B.C.

Mudaliyar an official, a chief of a division of a province.

Nāyaka lit. "leader," "guide," "chief." *Nāyaka Thera,* lit., "Leading Elder," is the official title of a Buddhist monk who is a provincial or regional Head of the *Sangha* (*q.v.*) within a certain geographical area in Ceylon. *Mahā Nāyaka Thera,* lit. "Great Leading Elder," is the official title of a Buddhist monk who is the Supreme Head of the *Sangha* of a *Nikāya* (*q.v.*) in the whole Island of Ceylon. *Anu-Nāyaka* is a Deputy Head of the *Sangha.*

Nāyaka Thera chief monk.

Nikāya "Collection" of discourses, sayings, utterances of the Buddha. The *Tipiṭaka* contains five *nikāyas.* Also a unit or sect of the *Sangha* (*q.v.*).

Nirvāṇa the Buddhist *summum bonum,* Ultimate Reality, Absolute Truth.

Pāli the ancient language, also called *Māgadhī* "the language of Magadha" in North India, in which the teaching of the Buddha is preserved according to the Theravāda (*q.v.*) tradition.

Pañca-sīla "The Five Precepts" for the lay Buddhist: abstention from 1) destroying life, 2) stealing, 3) adultery, 4) lying, and 5) intoxicating drinks.

Paṃsukūlika a Buddhist monk who takes the vow to wear only "rag robes," i.e. robes made from pieces of material discarded by people and thrown away into dust-bins and cemeteries.

Pariccāga giving up, renouncing.

Parinirvāṇa (Pāli: *Parinibbāna*) term used for the final passing away, the death, of a Buddha or a disciple who is an *arahant* (*q.v.*).

Pariyatti the Scriptures, the study of the Scriptures.

Paṭipatti practice, practicing and following the teaching.

Paṭivedha realization (of the Truth).

Pirit Sinhala word derived from Pāli *paritta,* lit. "protection." A *pirit* ceremony consists in the recitation by a group of *bhikkhus* (rarely by one *bhikkhu*) of selected *suttas* (*q.v.*) from the *Tipiṭaka* (*q.v.*) and of Pāli verses to confer protection and blessings on one or more persons.

Pirivena a Buddhist monastic institute where not only monks but also lay students are admitted and follow courses of study. A *pirivena* may be of college level or of lower school level. They are all attached to a temple or a monastery. The two leading Ceylon *pirivenas,* Vidyodaya and Vidyālaṅkāra, were granted university status in 1959.

Piṭaka Canon, scripture. Early Orientalists in the West translated this term, and some scholars still translate it, as "basket," taking its literal meaning ignoring the idiomatic usage. The expression *piṭaka-sampadāna* or *piṭaka-sampadā* means "canonical tradition," "scriptural tradition," and not "basket tradition!" See also *Tipiṭaka.*

Rālahāmy (*Rālahāmi*) a minor official. Also used today as a courtesy title in addressing a police constable.

Sangha the community of Buddhist monks.

Sangha-sabhā the Assembly or Council of the *Sangha.*

Samajīvikatā living within one's means.

Samānattatā equality.

Sāmaṇera a novice (monk).

Samantapāsādikā the Commentary on the *Vinaya-piṭaka* (*q.v.*).

Saṃsāra lit. "faring on," "moving on." Continued cycle of births and deaths; unbroken continuity of the Five Aggregates (*khandha*) (*rupa* "matter," *vedanā* "feelings," *saññā* "perceptions," *saṃkhāra* "mental formations" and *viññāṇa* "consciousness") which constitute a living being.

Samyakdṛṣti Right View.

Sāriputta the chief disciple of the Buddha.

Sāsana lit. "message," "teaching." The Message of the Buddha, the Doctrine and Discipline of the Buddha. Popularly: Buddhism, Buddhist religion.

Sīla virtue, moral precepts.

Sutta (Skt. *sūtra*) a discourse, a sermon.

Sutta-piṭaka "The Canon of the Discourses." The group of canonical Pāli texts containing the discourses, dialogues, sermons, sayings, utterances of the Buddha.

Tapa austerity.

Thera an elder, a senior monk.

Thera-vāda "The Teaching of the Elders," considered to be the earliest form of Buddhism now prevalent in Ceylon, Burma, Thailand, Cambodia, Laos, Chittagong, and some regions of India.

Tirinanxe wrong orthography of the word *terunnānse* which means "the Ven. Elder," "the Ven. *Thera.*"

Tissamahārāma the most venerated Buddhist monastery in the south of Ceylon, built about the 2nd century B.C.

Tipiṭaka (Skt. *Tripiṭaka*) "Triple Canon." Three main divisions or groups of the Buddhist Scriptures (generally translated as Three "Baskets!"), namely, 1) *Sutta-piṭaka* (*q.v.*), 2) *Vinaya-piṭaka* (*q.v.*) and 3) *Abhidhamma-piṭaka* (*q.v.*). See also *Piṭaka*.

Tripiṭakavāgīśvarācārya lit. "Supreme Master of the *Tripiṭaka*," highest and most distinguished honorary title conferred by a Chapter of the Order of the *Sangha* (*q.v.*) in recognition of great erudition and proficiency in the Buddhist Canonical and Commentarial literature. Not more than three (or four) persons hold this title in Ceylon at a time.

Upasampadā Higher Ordination of a Buddhist monk. The primary ordination as a *sāmaṇera* (novice) is called *pabbajjā* "going forth."

Uṭṭhānasampadā alertness, skill, efficiency in one's profession.

Vaitulyavāda heresy, heretical view.

Vaitulyavādin a heretic.

Vibhaṅga one of the seven books of the *Abhidhamma-piṭaka* (*q.v.*).

Vihāra monastery, temple. In popular usage today in Ceylon this term refers to the "image-house," the building where the image of the Buddha is installed and venerated.

Vinaya "Discipline."

Vinaya-piṭaka "The Canon of the Discipline." The division of the Buddhist Scriptures containing 5 books of the disciplinary rules (Canon Law) for the order of monks and nuns.

Vipassanā-dhura duty of meditation, occupation of meditation, responsibility of meditation, *Vipassanā*-meditation, Insight-meditation (*vipassanā* "insight," "insight-meditation," *dhura* "duty," "occupation"). Cf. *gantha-dhura.*

ABBREVIATIONS FOR NOTES

A *Aṅguttara-nikāya,* ed. Śrī Devamitta, Colombo.

AA *Aṅguttara-nikāyaṭṭhakathā* (*Manorathapūraṇī*), Commentary on the A (Simon Hewavitarne Publication, Colombo, Part I, 1923; Part II, 1931).

A.C. After Christ.

B.C. Before Christ.

D *Dīgha-nikāya* (Manutunga Publication, Colombo, 1929).

DA *Dīgha-nikāyaṭṭhakathā* (*Sumaṅgalavilāsinī*), Commentary on the D (Simon Hewavitarne Publication, Colombo, 1918).

Dhp *Dhammapada,* ed. K. Dhammaratana (Maha Bodhi Press, Colombo, 1926).

DhpA *Dhammapadaṭṭhakathā,* Commentary on the Dhp. (Simon Hewavitarne Publication, Part I, 1919; Part II, 1922).

EZ Epigraphia Zeylanica (Oxford University Press, London).

M *Majjhima-nikāya,* ed. K. Ñāṇavimala, Colombo.

MA *Majjhima-nikāyaṭṭhakathā* (*Papañcasūdanī*), Commentary on the M (Aluvihara ed., Part I, 1917; Part II, 1926).

Mhv *Mahāvaṃsa,* ed. Śrī Sumaṅgala and Baṭuvantuḍāve (Government Press, Colombo, 1908).

NOTES

PREFACE TO THE SECOND SINHALA EDITION

1 The organization of Buddhist monks, established on May 11, 1946, with a view to lead public opinion about religious, social, economic, and political questions. The author was mainly responsible for the creation of this organization, and was its first secretary-general.

CHAPTER 1

1 "*Caratha bhikkhave cārikaṃ bahujanahitāya bahujanasukhāya lokānukampāya atthāya hitāya sukhāya devamanussānaṃ.*" (*Mahāvagga*, p. 19). "Go ye, O *bhikkhus,* and wander forth for the good of the many, for the happiness of the many, in compassion for the world, for the welfare, for the good, for the happiness of gods and men."

2 Unjust trades are those that bring harm to other living beings such as trade in arms and lethal weapons, intoxicating drinks, poisons, killing animals, slave-traffic.

3 *Aṅguttara-nikāya,* pp. 69, 70.

4 *Ibid.,* pp. 232, 786.

5 *Dīgha-nikāya* (D), *Sigāla-sutta; Aṅguttara, Vyagghapajja-sutta.* (*Aṅguttara,* p. 788.)

6 *Aṅguttara,* p. 346.

7 *Parābhava-sutta, Sigāla-sutta,* etc.

8 *Dhammapada* (Dhp), verse 204; *Jataka* I, (PTS) p. 366.

9 *Aṅguttara,* p. 207.

10 *Dhammapadaṭṭhakathā* (DhpA) II, p. 592.

11 *Jātak* (PTS) I, 260, 399; II, 400; III, 274, 320; V, 119, 378.

12 *Dīgha* (D) II, *Mahāparinibbāna-sutta,* p. 44 f.

13 *Samantapāsādikā* I, p. 52; *Mahāvaṃsa,* Ch. I, v. 19 f.

14 *Samantapāsādikā* I, pp. 50–51.

CHAPTER 2

1 *Mahāvagga: Cīvarakkhandhaka.*

2 *Pācittiya: gaṇabhojanasikkhāpada.*

3 *Mahāvagga,* p. 242 ff.

4 *Ibid.,* p. 260 ff.

5 *Dīgha-nikāya* II, *Mahāparinibbāna-sutta,* p. 62.

6 *Ibid.,* p. 62.

7 Nalinaksh Dutt in *The Cultural Heritage of India,* Vol. I, p. 290.

8 *Dīgha,* II, p. 95.

CHAPTER 3

1 *Cullavagga: Pañcasatikakkhandhaka.*

2 The Vajji *bhikkhus* of Vesāli held that it was proper for a *bhikku*—

i. to keep salt in a horn vessel, in order to season unsalted foods, when received.

ii. to take the mid-day meal, even after the prescribed time, as long as the sun's shadow had not passed the meridian by more than two-fingers' breadth.

iii. to go into a village, after the meal, and eat there again, if invited.

iv. to hold the *uposatha* ceremony separately by *bhikkhus* living in a large monastery.

v. to carry out official acts of *Vinaya,* expecting to obtain afterwards the vote of the absent *bhikkhus.*

vi. to do something, whether proper or improper, because it was the preceptor's practice.

vii. to take unchurned milk even after meal-time.

viii. to drink unfermented palm wine.

ix. to use mats to sit on which were not of the prescribed size, if they were without fringe.

x. to accept gold and silver.

3 *Vinaya Piṭaka,* Vol. I, Introduction, p. XXIX.

4 *Samantapāsādikā* I, p. 19 ff. *Mahāvaṃsa,* Ch. iv.

5 *Mahāvaṃsa,* Ch. V, 1–13; *Nikāyasaṃgrahaya,* p. 5–6.

6 *Ceylon Lectures* (1945), p. 229.

7 *Samantapāsādikā* I, p. 37; *Mahāvaṃsa* xii, 1 ff.

CHAPTER 4

1 *Samantapāsādikā* I, p. 60.

2 The prevalence of this idea even during the Kandyan Period is shown by a letter sent by the British Governor Brownrigg to England dated 13th June 1816. This letter is given in another place of this book. See p. 86.

3 Epigraphia Zeylanica (EZ) I, pp. 234–237.

4 *Ibid.,* p. 234.

5 *Mahāvaṃsa* (Mhv) li 82.

6 EZ II, pp. 109, 159.

7 *Pūjāvaliya,* p. 656.

8 *Prabhāṣodaya,* 1930 May, p. 17.

9 Mhv xxxviii 38 *te maṃ vā sāsanaṃ vā no rakkhiṃsu.*

10 *Prabhāṣodaya,* 1930 May, p. 19.

11 EZ VI, p. 114 *budadasa ḷa parideva.*

12 King Śri Vijaya Rājasiṃha (1739–1747) was a Hindu prince from the Nayakkar clan in South India. Nevertheless, when he was crowned King of Ceylon he embraced the national religion of the people. Tamil kings who succeeded him likewise acted as Buddhists.

13 Mhv, xxxix 54.

CHAPTER 5

1 It should not be understood here that the *bhikkhus* went to fight in the war. Some are of the opinion that the *bhikkhus* were invited to go with the army in order that the warriors could offer them alms. Undoubtedly the *bhikkhus* were offered alms. However that is not the main import of the occasion. When *bhikkhus* accompany the army the war appears to be of religious significance, and more and more people support the war effort. The assistance of the *bhikkhus* was also necessary to establish peace and order in

the areas liberated. It is mentioned that King Rājasiṃha II (1635–1687 A.C.) took *bhikkhus* with him when he went to war. Mhv. xcvi 16.

2 Mhv. xxv 103–111.

3 Mhv. xxvii 9–20.

4 Mhv xxx 98.

5 *Ibid.* xxx 19–41.

6 *Ibid.* xxxiii 18.

7 *Ibid.* lxi 1–3.

8 *Davy's Travels in Ceylon* (London 1821), p. 159.

9 *A Sketch of the Constitution of the Kandyan Kingdom* by Sir John D'Oyly, Ceylon, 1929, p. 1.

CHAPTER 6

1 Mhv. xxxii 35–94.

2 *Vibhaṅgaṭṭhakathā*, pp. 314–318; *Aṅguttaraṭṭhakathā* (AA) p. 52.

3 AA, pp. 52–53.

4 AA, p. 53. *āraddhavipassakānaṃ bhikkhūnaṃ satepi sahasse'pi vijjamāne pariyattiyā asati ariyamaggapaṭivedho nāma na hoti.*

5 *Paṭivedho ca paṭipatti ca hotipi na hotipi, sāsanaṭṭhitiyā pariyatti pamāṇam. Paṇḍito hi tepiṭakam sutvā dvepi pūreti .... Tasmā pariyattiyā ṭhitāya sāsanaṃ ṭhitaṃ hoti.* DA, p. 654; MA II, p. 881.

6 *Vibhaṅgaṭṭhakathā*, p. 336.

7 Dhp I, 19–20.

8 Even to this day both these classes exist in Ceylon.

CHAPTER 7

1 Sometimes it is called *vāsa-dhura*. AA, I, p. 22.

2 A vague idea leading to this division may be conjectured in the classification of *pariyatti* (doctrine), *paṭipatti* (practice) and *paṭivedha* (realization, attainment). But it is not a division of vocations as study and meditation. There was no particular class of monks for study and for meditation. Study and meditation were meant for all.

3 *Dhammapadaṭṭhakathā*, p. 4. *Ahaṃ mahallakakāle pabbajito. Ganthadhuraṃ pūretuṃ na sakkhissāmi. Vipassanādhuraṃ pana pūressāmi.*

In the Commentary on the *Dhammapada* this is reported to have been uttered in the presence of the Buddha. But how could one speak of a vocation of scholarship which did not exist during the lifetime of the Buddha? It is therefore clear that this was written after the creation of the two vocations.

4 AA., p. 22. *Bhante, gantho nāma paṭibalassa bhāro. Mayhaṃ pana dukkhūpanisā saddhā. Vāsadhuraṃ pūressāmi.*

5 Even today there are some aged monks who spend their life in this manner.

6 EZ I, p. 85. The meaning of the word *vasag* has not yet been clearly known. However it signifies a payment in terms of food and clothing as indicated by the expressions "*kaňḍin piňḍin vasag.*"

7 The Päpiḷiyāna Inscription states that when a person who is learned in logic, grammar, etc., comes, he should be paid a salary and that monks should learn those subjects from him.

8 Mhv. xxxvii, 149, 150, 173; *Rasavāhinī*, ii, p. 77.

9 *Samantapāsādikā* I, p. 337.

10 *Ibid.* I, p. 220–221.

11 *Ibid.* I, p. 221. *Mayi sante bhikkhūnampi bhikkhunīnampi gihīnampi adhikaraṇaṃ ābhidhammika-Godattattherena vinicchitaṃ suvinicchitaṃ. Tassa vinicchaye atiṭṭhamānaṃ rājāṇāya ṭhapemi.*

12 Mhv. xxxiv, 66.

CHAPTER 8

1 EZ I, pp. 84–90; 4.

2 *Samantapāsādikā* 1, p. 338.

3 *Ibid.* 338–339.

4 *Dīgha-nikāyaṭṭhakathā* (DA) p. 717.

5 *Samantapāsādikā* III, p. 842.

6 D I, p. 49.

7 *Samantapāsādikā* III, p. 747. *vihāresu rājūhi ārāmikadāsā nāma dinnā honti, te'pi pabbājetuṃ na vaṭṭati, bhujisse katvā pana pabbājetuṃ vaṭṭati.*

8 *Majjhima-nikāyaṭṭhakathā* (MA) I, p. 404. *dāsidāsavasen'eva tesaṃ paṭiggahaṇaṃ na vaṭṭati; kappiyakārakaṃ dammi ārāmikaṃ dammīti evaṃ vutte pana vaṭṭati.*

9 EZ IV, pp. 132–135, 139–140, 144, 294–295; Mhv. xlvi 10; 164.

10 EZ IV, pp. 128, 144.

11 *Description of Ceylon* by James Cordiner, 1807, Vol. I, pp. 150–151.

12 Mhv xlii 23; EZ IV pp. 139–140.

13 EZ I pp. 4–5, 69, 84–90.

14 *A Sketch of the Constitution of the Kandyan Kingdom* by Sir John D'Oyly, Ceylon 1929, pp. 140–141.

CHAPTER 9

1 *Medieval Sinhalese Art,* p. 47.

2 The figures of door-keepers or guards at the entrance of a temple.

3 *Cullavagga,* p. 247; *Samantapāsādikā* IV, p. 900.

4 *Ceylon* by Sir James Emerson Tennent, Vol. I (London 1859), pp. 615, 620.

5 *Medieval Sinhalese Art,* pp. 47, 59, 168.

6 *Śrī Dharmāloka Caritaya,* p. 8 (1937) by Koṭahēnē Prajñākīrti. Today the Ven. Māpalagama Vipulasāra is well known as a distinguished sculptor-artist. He is the President of the National Arts Society of Ceylon.

7 *Dīgha-nikāyaṭṭhakathā,* p. 65.

8 *Dīpavamsa,* V 49.

9 *The Dīpavaṃsa and Mahāvaṃsa* by Wilhelm Geiger (Colombo, 1908), p. 1.

10 The *Mahāvaṃsa,* "The Great Chronicle of Ceylon," is

written in elegant Pāli verse, and has been continued up to the present century at different periods by Buddhist monks.

11 Martin Wickramasinghe, *Siṃhala Sāhityayē Nägīma,* p. 71.

CHAPTER 10

1 It is well known that King Siri Saṅgabō (Siri Sanghabodhi) (307–309 A.C.) received his education from his uncle Nanda Thera. King Kalikāla Sahitya-sarvajña Paṇḍita Parākramabāhu (1236–1271 A.C.) of Daṁbadeṇiya received his education from Sangharakkhita Thera (Mhv. lxxxi 76).

2 Mhv. xxxviii 14–37.

3 *Ibid.* xxxix 21.

4 *Ibid.* xxxix 29–31.

5 *Ibid.* lxviii 126–127.

6 *Ibid.* li 14.

7 *Ibid.* lii 9.

8 *Ibid.* liii 13 ff.

9 *Ibid.* lx 87.

10 *Ibid.* lxi 1–3.

11 *Ibid.* lxx 181; 328 ff; EZ IV, p. 6.

12 *Pūjāvaliya,* p. 689.

13 This king was well versed in Buddhism. He was a great scholar who wrote the *Viśuddhimārgasannaya* and the *Vinayaviniścayasannaya.*

14 Mhv. lxxxvii 39 ff.

15 *Katikāvat Saṅgarā,* introduction pp. v–vi by D. B. Jayatilaka.

16 This very valuable document preserved in the British Museum in London was copied by Sir D. B. Jayatilaka and reproduced in the *Prabhāṣodaya* 1930 April, May, June issues.

17 P. E. Pieris, *Tri Siṃhala,* 2nd ed., pp. 32–33.

CHAPTER 12

1 *Saṃgharāja Sādhucariyāva* (1916), p. 6.

CHAPTER 13

1 This is how the full name of the Ven. Vāriyapoḷa Thera is given in a deed preserved in the Huduhumpoḷa Temple in Kandy.

CHAPTER 14

1 L. A. Mills, *Ceylon Under the British Rule,* pp. 124–125.

2 *A History of Ceylon for Schools* by Father S. G. Perera, S.J. (1949), Part II, p. 112.

3 *A History of Ceylon Police,* Vol. I (Colombo), p. 180.

4 Nine monks headed by Girānegama Chandajoti Nāyaka Thera, having chanted *pirit* and conferred the merits on the gods, launched this rebellion against the English. A few days later these *bhikkhus* were taken prisoner by Malay soldiers in the pay of the British Government. On the morning of the day following their capture the Malay soldiers who were leading them handcuffed, put them into a waterlogged paddy field and gave them some rice hoppers (pancakes) to eat, which they had fetched from a nearby boutique. The *bhikkhus* refused to eat these hoppers saying: "We are not the kind of people who will eat food in this manner, which is against our custom." The Malay soldiers who did not know about the customs of *bhikkhus* asked them to explain. The *bhikkhus* said: "If the food is given to us after allowing us to wash our mouth and face and making us suitably seated, then only we will accept it. Otherwise even if we die of starvation we do not partake of any food offered to us in this improper manner." The soldiers said: "If we remove your handcuffs and allow you to do all that, you will run away from us." The *bhikkhus* replied: "We are not the people that will run away in fear." Thereupon the soldiers removed the handcuffs, allowed the *bhikkhus* to rinse their mouths and wash their faces, took them to the nearby boutique, made them sit on seats prepared for them and offered them their morning meal duly prepared. Until the case against them was heard, they were remanded in a *kachcheri* (administrative headquarters of a district). Since it was difficult to idle away the

time, one of the *bhikkhus* suggested that they chant *pirit* again. To this day the tradition has it that to this suggestion one of the *bhikkhus* remarked rather humorously: "We are in this plight today after chanting *pirit*!"

5 *A History of Ceylon for Schools* by Father S. G. Perera, S.J. (1943), Part II, p. 144 ff.

CHAPTER 15

1 As mentioned above, the British governed the maritime provinces at that time. Nevertheless the Sinhala people who lived in these areas were loyal to the Sinhala government in Kandy and opposed the British government. The main reason for this was Buddhism.

2 In ancient times every temple or monastery was a school where education was free. Monastic centers such as the Mahāvihāra at Anurādhapura were like universities.

3 See above, p. 32.

4 *Vedarāḷas* are physicians who are laymen.

5 *Medieval Sinhalese Art* by Ananda K. Coomaraswamy, p. 45.

6 *An Account of the Island of Ceylon* by Robert Percival, London, 1803, p. 201.

CHAPTER 16

1 Just as the English tried to destroy the political power of Buddhist monks in Ceylon, so did the Brahmins, during the time of Puṣyamitra, after the death of Asoka, try to destroy the political influence of Buddhist monks in India. (See *Glimpses of World History* by Jawaharlal Nehru, 3rd ed., 1945, p. 78.)

2 There was a rule during the Dutch period that no mudaliyarship be given to a native who did not belong to this Christian denomination. Therefore many a high class Sinhalese embraced Christianity in order to obtain these positions.

3 Note how the power of *bhikkhus* has been tapped for the advantage of the English Government.

4 *Bhikkhus* who are educated and who are of good conduct naturally enjoy a high degree of honor and respect in the country. The venture on the part of the Government to bestow them with honor is a part of the Government program to enlist their favor.

5 This leads to conflicts between the *mudaliyars* and the *bhikkhus* and to disunity among them.

6 Now it is crystal clear why the *bhikkhus* were baited with this high priesthood. Everybody knows the motives for conferring knighthoods by the English Government on influential Sinhalese laymen.

7 Even when the British Government prevailed over the maritime provinces, the investiture of *bhikkhus* with offices was performed by the two Chapters of Malvatta and Asgiriya in Kandy as well as by the government of the Kandyan Kingdom. The English wanted to stop this.

8 i.e. Malvatta and Asgiriya.

9 i.e. eight days after the Convention.

10 Later it will be clear why the government severed its connection with Buddhism.

11 An important incident comes to my mind as an illustration: On the Full-Moon Day of Durutu on January 6th, Monday, 1947, the Buddhist monks who assembled in Kälaṇiya Temple (Rāja Mahā Vihāra) made a historic Political Declaration on the Freedom of Ceylon. (See Appendix III.) A few days later the *mahā nāyaka theras* (high priests) of the Malvatta and Asgiriya Vihāras in Kandy wrote to the Governor of Ceylon saying that they were not in any way associated with that Declaration and that their loyalty to the English Government continued as before.

And further, when the Governor went to see the Tooth relic of the Buddha at the Temple of the Tooth relic in Kandy in January 1947, the two *mahā nāyaka theras* of Malvatta and Asgiriya met him there and re-affirmed their loyalty to the British Crown.

Sometime ago when the *mahā nāyaka thera* of Malvatta went before the non-Buddhist governor to receive his Act of Appointment the governor thanked him for being loyal to His Majesty the King and the British Government.

12 After this book was published (1st edition 1946 and 2nd edition 1948) people began to talk about the question of this Act of Appointment. It is gratifying to note here that those phrases requesting the recipient of the office of high priest to be loyal and faithful to the British Government and to do spying have now been removed from the Act of Appointment.

CHAPTER 17

1 While "encouragement to Buddhism" was stopped, in the same year the Diocesan Committee of Ceylon was established to spread Christianity.

2 *Ceylon Under the British Rule* by L. A. Mills, pp. 126–128.

3 It should be noted that Governor Mackenzie refused to sign the warrants appointing priests to temples. Thenceforth the chief incumbency of temples became confused.

4 See above, pp. 37–38, 70.

CHAPTER 18

1 At the beginning missionaries from Europe were paid by the government like civil servants. The Civil List of 1825 shows the salaries paid to missionaries. The British Government paid the salaries of missionaries because they were extremely helpful to them in running their colonial government.

2 It is evident that the protection given to the Buddhists was simply nominal.

3 It is interesting to note here that already in this letter the expression "the Superstition of Boodhoo" is used for "the Religion of Boodhoo" in the 5th Article of the Convention.

CHAPTER 19

1 A recent incident comes to my mind as an illustration. Presiding at the Prize Giving of the Good Shepherd's Convent in Colombo on March 8, 1947, Dr. J. M. Masson, the Archbishop of Colombo, earnestly advised the Sinhalese and the Tamil children to abandon their "queer names" and to

use the names of the Catholic Saints. What he termed "queer names" are Sinhalese and Tamil national names. The names he advocated are foreign Christian names. This is how children were taught to despise their own culture and to adore the western culture. (See *Sunday Observer,* March 9, 1947.)

2 It is gratifying to note here that many Ceylonese Christians are now realizing their past mistakes and are beginning to appreciate and accept national traditions, customs, and institutions.

CHAPTER 20

1 Now Vidyodaya University of Ceylon.

2 Now Vidyālaṅkāra University of Ceylon.

3 This school which still exists was afterwards handed over to the Buddhist Theosophical Society in Colombo for management. See *Kalyāṇi śāsana vaṃsaya,* p. 129.

4 It is still one of the leading colleges in Ceylon.

5 The Sinhalese Buddhists commemorate Col. H. S. Olcott on February 17th annually, and in his memory a principal street in Colombo, with his statue, is named "Olcott māvata."

6 In ancient times all languages, arts and sciences were taught in the monasteries. The Päpiḷiyāna Inscription states that whenever educated people were available, they should even be paid for and their knowledge acquired. At present the very poor financial conditions of the *pirivenas* do not permit them to hire teachers.

7 It should be noted that in those difficult days, Principal P. de S. Kularatne of Ānanda College and Principal J. E. Gunasekara of Mahābodhi College provided opportunities for and encouraged *bhikkhus* to study English and other modern subjects at Ānanda College and Mahābodhi College.

POSTSCRIPT

1 E. F. C. Ludowyk: *The Modern History of Ceylon,* (Frederick A. Praeger, New York, 1966) p. 204.

2 We come across a similar episode in Ceylon history as

early as the 1st century A.C. About 60 *bhikkhus* at Mihintalē who plotted to assassinate King Kaṇirajānu-Tissa (89–92 A.C.) over a monastic dispute were ordered to be thrown from a high rock. After this terrible incident, Mihintalē, which was always highly venerated, seemed to have become unpopular for a fairly long period. See Walpola Rāhula, *History of Buddhism in Ceylon* (M. D. Gunasena & Co. Ltd., Colombo, 1966, 2nd ed.) pp. 86–87.

3 *E.g.,* A Marxist minister of the present government, asked in London by a B.B.C. reporter whether those young people who rebelled in April 1971, were not educated in universities, replied with an air of contempt: "Yes, through the Sinhalese medium." This was not published in Ceylon, as it was censored by the government.

4 A vivid account of events during this period is given in a series of four excellent articles by Jacques Decornoy in *Le Monde,* Paris, June 16, 17, 18, 19, 1971.

APPENDIX I

1 See Yagirala Paññānanda Nāyaka Thera's articles in the *Siḷumiṇa,* May 19, 1946; the *Dinamiṇa,* March 29, 1946.

2 See Yagirala Paññānanda Nāyaka Thera's article in the *Siḷumiṇa,* May 19, 1946.

3 The *Dinamiṇa,* March 7, 1946.

4 *Everybody's Political What's What,* p. 353.

5 "The Ten Duties of the King" (*dasa-rājadhamma*) are: (1) *dāna:* liberality, generosity, charity; (2) *sīla:* morality; (3) *pariccāga:* sacrificing everything for the good of the people; (4) *ajjava:* honesty, integrity; (5) *maddava:* gentleness, kindness; (6) *tapa:* austerity, simplicity in life; (7) *akkodha:* freedom from hatred, ill-will, enmity; (8) *avihiṃsā:* non-violence, promote peace preventing violence and war; (9) *khanti:* patience, forbearance, tolerance, understanding; (10) *avirodha:* non-opposition, non-obstruction, should not oppose the will of the people, should not obstruct measures conducive to the welfare of the people..

A letter to the Dutch Governor Falk in Colombo (1760 A.C.) sent by the Malvatta Chapter in Kandy says that the control of the five sense faculties is fundamental for good government and that a country should be ruled according to "The Ten Duties of the King." (The *Prabhāṣodaya,* April 1930, pp. 15–16.)

6 "The Four Qualities of Benevolence" (*cattāri saṅgahavatthūni*) are: (1) *dāna,* liberality, generosity, charity; (2) *peyyavajja,* kindly speech; (3) *atthacariyā,* a life of service; (4) *samānattatā,* equality, impartiality.

7 *Devo vasstu kālena, sassasampattihetu ca,*
phīto bhavatu loko ca, rājā bhavatu dhammiko.

May there be rain in season
To yield a rich harvest,
May the world be prosperous,
And may the ruler(s) be righteous.

This verse, which may be considered as the Buddhist anthem, contains the social, economic, and political aspirations.

8 *Manusmrti,* VII, 2–3.

9 Aristotle's *Politica,* I, 2.

10 *Social Evolution and Political Theory* (N.Y. 1922), p. 184.

11 *Political Ideals* (OUP 1915), p. 292.

12 *Ibid.,* p. 295.

13 *Everybody's Political What's What,* p. 364.

14 *An Introduction to Politics,* London, 1931, p. 15.

15 *Politica,* I, 1.

16 *A Grammar of Politics,* London, 1925, p. 37.

17 *Ibid.,* p. 37.

18 *Political Ideals,* p. 294.

19 Today in Ceylon there are about 20,350 *bhikkhus;* of these about 600 are forest-dwellers (*vana-vāsī* or *arañña-vāsī*); there are 6,561 Buddhist temples and monasteries.

20 The *Times of Ceylon,* which is owned by some Christian Englishmen, laments that the purity of Buddhism will be polluted by the *bhikkhus* taking to politics (editorial, February 20, 1946). Those who have by now read the sections describing the happenings in this country after

British occupation will understand this sudden devotion of these gentlemen to protect the purity of Buddhism.

21 Even today there are some people who are against the Buddhist monks receiving a modern education.

22 Nevertheless several *nāyaka theras* are appointed patrons or advisers of these various societies and associations. At the annual general meeting of each of these one of the *nāyaka theras*—a patron or adviser—is respectfully invited to attend. He is seated on a chair spread with a white cloth respectfully. The members of the association take the five precepts (*pansil*) from him and listen with great devotion to a sermon delivered by him. The *nāyaka thera's* patronage for a whole year is limited to this service! Neither in the important issues before the association nor in the matters of settling the diverse disputes in the association is he consulted by the members. The innocent *nāyaka thera,* too, is quite satisfied with what patronage he is supposedly contributing. He does not realize that this patronage is meaningless.

Buddhist leaders always declare that *bhikkhus* are their advisers and patrons. Yet they do not get any advice from them on any important issue. Sometime ago, when the Buddhist Theosophical Society was thrown into confusion and disorder, there was neither consultation of patrons and advisers nor was their available advice adhered to. The Buddhist leaders headed by the Hon. Mr. D. S. Senanayake did not consult the *bhikkhus'* point of view whether it was good or bad to accept the Soulbury Constitution and later the Dominion Status which determined the future happiness or unhappiness of millions of Ceylonese.

BIBLIOGRAPHY

PĀLI

Aṅguttara-nikāya (Śrī Devamitta, ed., Colombo)

Cullavagga (Saddhātissa, ed., Alutgama, 1915)

Dīgha-nikāya (Manatunga Publication, Colombo, 1929)

Dīpavaṃsa (Ñāṇānanda, ed., Star Press, Panadure, 1927)

Dhammapada (K. Dhammaratana, ed., Mah Bodhi Press, Colombo, 1926); (tr. F. Max Mueller, Dover, N.Y.)

Dhammapadaṭṭhakathā (Simon Hewavitarne Publication, Part I, 1919; Part II, 1922)

Majjhima-nikāya (Ñaṇavimala, ed., Colombo)

Manorathapūraṇī (Simon Hewavitarne Publication, Part I, 1923; Part II, 1931)

Mahāvagga (Saddhātissa, ed., Alutgama, 1922)

Mahāvaṃsa (Śrī Sumaṅgala and Baṭuwantudāve, eds., Government Press, Colombo, 1908)

Mahāvaṃsa (Yagirala Paññānanda, 1935) Part III

Papañcasūdanī (Aluvihara, ed., Part I, 1917; Part II, 1926)

Pācittiya (Ariyavaṃsa, ed., Colombo B. E. 2472)

Rasavāhinī II (Jinālaṅkāra Press, B. E. 2464)

Samantapāsādikā (Simon Hewavitarne, ed., 1929)

Sammohavinodanī (Simon Hewavitarne, ed., 1932)

Suttanipāta, P. T. S. (tr. F. Max Mueller, Dover, N.Y.)

Sumaṅgalavilāsinī (Simon Hewavitarne, ed., 1918)

Vaṃsatthappakāsinī (*Mahāvaṃsa-ṭīkā*) (Malalasekera, ed., Parts I & II P.T.S.)

Vinaya (Oldenberg ed., 5 vols. P.T.S.; tr. B. Horner, *The Book of the Discipline*, 6 vols. Sacred Books of the Buddhists Series)

SANSKRIT

Bodhicaryāvatāra (M. Sāsanaratana, ed., Colombo)

Manusmṛti (Nirnaya-sagara Press, Bombay)

SINHALA

Dharmapradīpikā (Śrī Dharmārāma, ed., 1915)

Katikāvat-saṅgarāva (Jayatilaka, ed., 1922)

Kalyāṇisāsanavaṃsaya (Polwatte Śrī Buddhadatta, 1935)

Laṅkā-itihāsaya, early period (Mendis, 1942)

Nikāya-saṅgrahaya (Ceylon Government Press, 1907)

Pūjāvaliya (Jinālaṅkāra Press, Colombo, 1926)

Saṅgharāja Sādhu Cariyāva (Laṅkāloka Press, Galle, 1916)

Siṃhala Sāhityayē Nägīma (Martin Wickramasinghe, 1945)

Śrī Dharmāloka Caritaya (Koṭahēnē Paññākitti, 1937)

ENGLISH

A Short History of the World, H. G. Wells (London, 1927)

A Sketch of the Constitution of the Kandyan Kingdom, Sir John D'Oyly (Ceylon, 1929)

Grammar of Politics, Harold J. Laski (Humanities Press, New York, 1967)

A History of Ceylon for Schools, I & II, Father S. G. Perera, S.J., (Colombo, 1943)

A History of the Ceylon Police I, (Colombo)

An Introduction to Politics, Harold J. Laski (London, 1931)

Ceylon Under British Rule 1795–1932, Lennox A. Mills (Barnes & Noble, New York, 1965)

Ceylon, Sir James Emerson Tennent (London, 1859)

Ceylon Lectures, B. M. Barua (Calcutta, 1945)

Davy's Travels in Ceylon (London, 1821)

A Description of Ceylon, James Cordiner (1807) (AMS Press, New York)

Epigraphia Zeylanica, Parts I, II, III, IV

Everybody's Political What's What, Bernard Shaw (London, 1944)

Glimpses of World History, Jawaharlal Nehru (Asia Publishing House, New York)

Medieval Sinhalese Art, Ananda K. Coomaraswamy, the original ed. of 1908 or 2nd ed. revised, published by Pantheon Books, New York, with the patronage of the Government of Ceylon, 1956

Political Ideals, C. Delisle Burns (O.U.P., 1915)

Social Evolution and Political Theory, Leonard T. Hobhouse (Kennikat Press, Port Washington, New York, 1968)

Theories and Forms of Political Organizations, G. D. H. Cole

Tri Siṃhala, P. E. Pieris (Second ed., Ceylon, 1939)

INDEX

Abhaya (marauder), 35
Abhaya (Thera), Dīgha-bhāṇaka, chief incumbent of Mihintalē, 35, 36
Abhayagiri Vihāra, 25
Abhidhamma, 3
Abhidhamma Piṭaka, 30, 31
Act of Appointment of chief monks, xxv, 75, 76, 77, 78, 159, 160
ajjava, 6
akkodha, 6
All Ceylon Buddhist Congress, *see* Buddhist Congress
Aluvihāra, 26
Amaravaṃsa, Telvattē Śrī, xxiii
Ambulugala, 55
America, 100, 106
anāmaṭṭha-piṇḍapāta, 35
anaṇasukha, 4
Ānanda, 11, 12, 13
Ānanda College, 94, 161, 162
anātma, 138
anatta, 29
anavajjasukha, 4
Aṅguttara-nikāya, Commentary to, 26
anicca, 29
Anurādhapura, 24, 25, 33, 91, 102
Anuruddha, Kākkapalliyē, xvii
arahants, 22
  of Piyaṅgudīpa, 21
Arakan, 59
ārakkhasampadā, 4
araṇyavāsī (forest-dwellers), 28
Aristotle, 123, 124
Asgiriya, 38, 75, 78, 98, 159
Asia, 106, 111
asiggāhaka, 19
Asoka (Emperor), 14, 15, 16, 123, 158
atthacariyā, 5
atthisukha, 4
Avanti (kingdom), 9, 10
avihiṃsā, 6
avirodha, 6
Āyurveda Saṅgamaya, 104
Āyurvedic College, 109
āyurvedic medicines, 100

Badulla, 55
Bālāvabodhana, 28
Bämiṇiṭiyā sāya (famine), 24, 25, 26
Bandaranaike, S. W. R. D., 103, 104
  created Ministry of Culture, 105
  assassinated, 108
Bangla Desh, 110
Baptists, 87
Barnes, Edward (Governor), 83
Barua, B. M., 14
Bases of Assistance, four, 5
Basnayaka, Hema, 109
Bathurst, Lord (Secretary of State for the Colonies), 75, 83, 84
Bauddha Mandiraya (Buddhist Theosophical Society Head Quarters), xx
Bēruvala, 56
Bhāṣā Peramuṇa, 104
Bhātiya (King), 33
Bhesajjakkhandhaka, 10
Bhesajjamañjūsā, 32
bhikkhus, 28, 29, 39, 51, 57, 109 and *passim*
  accompanying army, 21
  skilled in architecture, 22
  as artists, 40 f.
  associated with JVP, 116
  attracted to social reform and welfare activities, 99 f.
  their civil rights denied, 118
  and commonplace talk, 42
  their deterioration, 91 f.
  dhammakathika, 26, 27, 28
  engaged in educational and social activities, 108
  higher education, 108
  influenced by modern trends, 108

bhikkhus (cont.)
knew and practiced medicine, 31 f.
opened *pirivenas,* 94
paṃsukūlika, 26, 27, 28
and politics, 125 f., 131
population of, 127
rebellions under the leadership of, 66 f.
salaries to, 38
as teachers, 31
of weak intelligence, 30
why well looked after, 39
a *bhikkhu* of position equal to Chief Justice, 33
Bhikṣuvagē Urumaya, xxi
bhogasukha, 4
Bible, translation of the, 83
Blake, William, 123
bohdi, 138
Bombay, 63
Boodhoo, the Religion of, 79, 83
superstition of, 84
Boston Museum, 40
Bo tree, 18, 19
Bōvala Thera, 71
British, 63, 64, 66, 68, 71, 79, 80, 82
Brownrigg (Governor), 75, 83, 84, 86, 152
Buddha, 3–13 *passim,* 15, 18, 22, 26, 36, 38, 40, 41, 42; his attention to government, 5
Buddhaghosa, 34, 42
Buddha Jayanti, 100; and Buddhist reawakening, 106
Buddharakkhita, Māpiṭigama, 103, 108
Buddha Sāsana Commission, 107
Buddha Sāsana Council, 101
Buddha Sāsana Samiti, 103
Buddhism, 56, 118 and *passim*
in decline, 59
Encyclopaedia of, 106
and politics, 122 f.
taking firm root in a country, 16, 17
Buddhist Committee of Inquiry, 104, 107; its report and recommendations, 101
Buddhist Congress, All Ceylon, 100, 101, 130
Buddhist monasteries (temples), as free schools, 31; male and female servants in, 37 f.
Buddhist temporalities, confusion of, 79 f.
Buddhist Theosophical Society, 94, 129, 161
Buddhoo, 73
Buddhoo Priests, 72, 74
Budha Religion, 85
Burma, 40, 57, 101, 107, 110
Burns, Delisle, 124, 125

Cakkavattisīhanāda-sutta, 3
Cakkhupāla (Elder), 30
Calcutta, 63
Calvert, Sir Henry, 86, 87
Cambodia, 101, 107, 110
Camden, Lord, 68, 83
Candy (Kandy), 68, 69, 70, 74
Canterbury, 9
Caratotta, Caratotta Tiroon Wahansa (Karatoṭa Terun Vahansē), 73, 74
Castlereagh, Lord, 83
Cetiya (*dāgäba*), 35
Ceylon (Lankā), 6, 7, 16, 17, 19, 23, 24, 39, 40, 50, 53, 55, 58, 61, 63, 64, 69, 101, 106, 109, 110 and *passim. See also* Laṅkā and Śrī Laṅkā
atrocities and cruelties, 117
Civil Rights Movement, 118
Committee in London, 118
emergency regulations, 116
became independent, 98
declared Republic of Śrī Laṅkā, 118
unemployment in, 113
Chandajoti, Girānegama Chandajoti, 66, 157
Chandaratana, Labuhēngoḍa, xvii
chaṭṭha-saṅgāyanā, see Sixth Council
China, 40, 41, 109, 110
People's Republic of, 116
Chola, 17, 20
Christianity, 61, 118
Christian missionaries, 79, 83
imported from Europe, 82
services of, 83
Christian schools, 82
Church of England, 87
cinnamon trade, 61
Colepepper, John S., 66
Colombo, 63, 66, 93, 100
Communist Party (C.P.), 29, 113, 114
Coomaraswamy, Ananda K., 40, 158

Cordinar, James, 73, 155
Council, first, 13; second, 14; third, 14; sixth, 100
Cullvagga, 40

dāgäba, 18, 41
daham pāsal (schools for teaching Buddhism to children) 105, 106
Daṁbadeṇiya, 48, 156
Daṁbulla, Daṁbulla Rock Temple, 66
dāna, 5, 6
dasarājadhamma, 6
Decornoy, Jacques, 162
Degaldoruva, 41
Description of Ceylon, 37
De Zoysa, A.P., xx
Devānampiya-Tissa, 16
Devaragampala Silvatanne Unnanse, 41
Devundara, 55
Dhamma, 11, 13, 14, 21, 27, 29
Dhammakkhandha, Moratoṭa Rājaguru (negotiates a trade pact), 54
Dhammāloka, Hīnaṭiyana, 99, 100
Dhammapada, 27
Dhammapadaṭṭhakathā, 5
Dhanapala, D. B., xiii, xiv, xxiii, xxv
dharma, 138
Dharmāloka College, xxv
Dharmāloka, Ratmalānē Śrī, 42, 93
Dharmapāla, Anagārika, 94
Dhātusena, 18, 50, 51
Dias, N. Q., 103
Dīgha-nikāya, 3, 4
  Commentary to, 27, 36
Dīpaṅkara (Buddha), 3
Dīpaṅkara, Vāriyapola, *see* Vāriyapola Thera
Dīpavaṃsa, 48
Doḍanduva, 93
D'Oyly, Sir John, 38, 153, 155
dukkha, 29, 137, 138
  the arising of, the cessation of, the Path leading to the cessation of, 137
Dutch, 58, 59, 60, 61, 63, 64, 69, 73
Duties of the King, ten, 6, 122, 162, 163
Dutt, N., 14
Duṭṭhagāmaṇī, *see* Duṭugämuṇu
Duṭugämuṇu (Duṭṭhagāmaṇī), 20, 21, 22, 23
  Arahants consoling, 21

earnings, how to use, 4
Eden (Government Agent of Mātara District), 68, 72
Eksat Bhikṣu Maṇḍalaya (United Bhikkhu Council), xxi, 103
Eksat Bhikṣu Peramuṇa, 103, 104
Eḷāra, 20
Eminent Indians, xiii, xiv
Encyclopaedia of Buddhism, see Buddhism
England, 68, 106, 116
English, 63, 66, 68, 71, 79
  Government, 75
Europe, 100, 106

Falk (Dutch Governor), 18, 53, 163
family prosperity, 5
free education, 111, 133
French, 58

Gajabāhu, 52, 53
Galle, 54, 56, 73
Gampola, 55
gaṇa-bhojana, 9
gandhakuṭi, 136
Gandhi, Mahatma, 122, 123
gantha-dhura, xxii, 29, 31, 33
Gäṭaṁbe Ford, 57
gāthā, 48
gāvuta, 36
Geiger, Wilhelm, 48, 155
Germany, East, 114
Godatta Thera, Ābhidhammika, 33
Godhagatta-Tissa, 20
Good Shepherd's Convent, 161
Gotama, the Buddha, 3
government, the Buddha's attention to, 5
grāmavāsī (village-dwellers), 28
Guṇānanda, Migeṭṭuvattē Śrī, 93
Guṇaratana, Attuḍāvē, xvii
Gunasekara, J. E., 161

Hambugallaka (Kemgalu), 24
happiness, four kinds of, 4
Harischandra, Brahmacārī Valisingha, 94
Hawaii, 110

health, 5, 6
higher education, 59
Hīnaṭiyana, 100
Hinduism, 56, 118
History of Buddhism in Ceylon, 140, 143, 162
Hobart, Lord, 63
Hobhous, Dr., 124
Hong Kong, 110
Huduhumpola Temple, Huduhumpola Royal Temple, 65, 157

India, 6, 53, 101, 106, 110, 116
Islam, 118
Israel, 114

Jaffna, 55, 63
Janatā Vimukti Peramuṇa (J.V.P.), People's Liberation Front, 115, 116
Japan, 40, 101, 106, 110, 111
jātaka (birth stories of the Buddha), 40, 41
Java, 40
Jayabāhu, 52
Jayatilaka, D. B., 156
Jesus Christ, 56
Jesus of Nazareth, 92
Jetavana Sanskrit Inscription, 34
jeṭmavak, 37
Jīvaka, 8
Jñānānanda, Mādōviṭa Śrī, xxvi
Johnson, Dr., 120, 121
Jövendö (Hungarian Weekly), xxi

Kachcheri, 90
Kakusandha (Buddha), 6
Kälaṇiya, xxv, 134
Kāḷāsoka, 14
kalyāṇamittatā, 4
Kalyāṇi sāmagrī saṅgha sabhā, 102
kammaṭṭhāna, 48
Kandy, xxv, 18, 19, 37, 42, 54, 56, 60, 63, 64, 72, 74, 75, 76, 77, 78, 98
  Chapter, 77
  school for teaching English, 88
Kandyan Convention, 64, 75, 79, 81, 83, 84, 88
  Article 5, 98
  Article 5 and its interpretation, 83 f.
Kandyan Districts, 66
Kandyan Kingdom, 38, 85
  independence of the, and Buddhism, 89
  19th century society in the, 69
Kandyan Provinces, 57
Kandyans, confined to barbarous ignorance, 88
Kaṇirajānu-Tissa, 162
Karatoṭa Thera, 71
karuṇā, 5
Kassap (Buddha), 7
Kassapa (King), 51
Kassapa IV, 52
Kassapa (Dr. Cassius A. Pereira), xxii
Kataragama, 30, 102
katikāvat, 28
Kerala, 17
khanti, 6
khuddānukhuddaka-sikkhāpada, 13
Khuddapārinda, 19
Kīrti Śrī Rājasiṃha, 60, 63
Koṇāgamana (Buddha), 6
Korea, North Korea, 110, 114
Kaṭahēna, xix
Kotalawala, Sir John, 103
Kotte, 49, 55
Kotte Chapter, 102
Kuḍāpola Thera, 66, 75
  shot dead in his yellow robes, 67, 78
Kularatna, P. de S., 161
Kūṭadanta-sutta, 3
Kuṭhāri (Monastery), 51

lābha-sīmā "revenue-boundary," 36
Lajji-Tissa, 23
Lak-sala, 105
Lankā, 6, 18, 91, 118, *see also* Ceylon *and* Śrī Laṅkā
Laṅkāputra Press, xxiii
Laṅkā Sama Samāja Party (L.S.S.P.), 113, 114
Laos, 107, 110
Laski, Harold, 124, 125
Licchavi, Licchavi Republic, 6
Lohapāsāda, 22
London, 105
London University, 111, 124
Ludowyk, E. F. C., xviii, 162

Mackenzie (Governor), 80, 160
Mādampe, 55
maddava, 6

Madras, 63
Magadha, 6
Maggona, 56
Mahābodhi College, 161, 162
Mahā-Kaccāyana (Elder), 9
mahā-karuṇā, 137
Mahā-Kāśyapa, Dim̐bulāgala, 28
Mahānāma, 22, 42, 50
Mahānāma, Kaluvachchimullē, xvii
Mahāpaduma Thera, 32
mahā-prajñā, 137
Maha Saman Dēvālaya, 102
Mahāsammata, King, 48
Mahāsaṅghika, Sect, 14
Mahā-Tissa, Thera, 24
Mahāvagga, 10
Mahavāli River, 57
Mahāvaṃsa, 17, 22, 33, 37, 42, 48, 50, 51, 123
Mahāvihāra, 25, 33, 51, 158
Mahāyāna, 110, 137
Mahinda (son of Asoka), 16, 17
Mahinda II, 51
Mahinda IV, 17, 30, 34
Mahinda, Ādipāda, 52
Mahinda, Viceroy, 52
Maitland (Governor), 68, 71, 72, 74, 83
Majjhima-nikāya, Commentary to, 27, 37
Malalasekera, Gunapāla *or* G. P., xxv, 100
Malaysia, 106, 110
Māligākanda, 93
Malvatta (in Kandy), 38, 42, 75, 76, 78, 98, 159, 163
  Chapter, xxv, 18, 54, 122
Mānābharaṇa, 52
Maṇḍalagiri Vihāra, 53
Mañjuśrī, Thera, 105
Manusmṛti, 123
Maritime Provinces, 58
Marxist, 103, 113
  leaders, 113, 115, 116
  minister, 162
  parties, 113
Masson, Dr. J. M. (Archbishop of Colombo), 161
Mātalē, 26
Mātara, 71
Matura (Mātara), 72, 73
Mayūrapāda Pirivena, 32
McCartney, Lord, 63
Mid-Country, 10
Migeṭṭuvattē, *see* Guṇānanda
Mihintalē, 35, 162
  female servants in, 37
  Slab Inscription, 30, 34
Milakkha-Tissa, 30
Mills, L. A., 66, 79, 160
minor rules, 13
missionaries, influence and activities, 90 f.
  salaries paid to, 160
Modaliyars (Mudaliyars), 68, 72, 73, 74
Moggallāna, King, 19, 51
Mookirigala, 73
Moratoṭa Mahā Nāyaka Thera, 42
Mudaliyar, 61, 71

Ñāṇasīha, Hēnpiṭagedara, 103
Ñāṇāvāsa, Hēnpiṭagedara, xvii
Nanda (artist monk), 41
Nanda (Thera, King Siri Saṅgabo's uncle), 156
Nandasāra, Gallāllē, xxiii
Nārada, xxii
National Arts Society of Ceylon, 105
nāyaka theras, 23, 38
Nayakkar, 152
Negambo, 63
Nehru, Jawaharlal, 158
Nepal, 101
nikāyas, 109
nirvāṇa, 3, 26, 131 and *passim*
Nissaṅkamalla, 17
North, Frederic (Governor), 68, 83
North Britain (newspaper), 120
Northwestern University, xi, xvii, xviii

Olcott, Colonel Henry Steel (H. S.), 94, 129, 161
Oldenberg, Hermann, 14

Paddy Lands Bill, 104
Pakistan, 116
Pali Canon, 17, 34
Pali Commentaries, 34
Pāliyagoḍa, xix, 42, 93
Pānadura, 56
Paññākara, Nāttaṇḍiyē, xvii, xxvi
Paññānanda, Yagirala, 162
Paññāsāra, K., 133
Paññāsekhara, Kalukaňdayāvē, 99
Pansala, 69
Päpiḷiyana Inscription, 154, 161
Parābhava-sutta, 5

Parākramabāhu I (Great), 52, 53
Parākramabāhu, Kalikāla Sāhitya-sarvajña Paṇḍita, 53, 156
Parākramabāhu VI (Śrī Parākramabāhu), 53
Parama Dhamma Chetiya Pirivena, 93, 105
Paramadhamma-cetiyārāma, 93
Parama Dhamma Chetiya Temple, 105, 110
Paraṇavitāna, S., 53
pariccāga, 6
parinirvāṇa, 11, 12, 13
pariyatti, 26
Parliament, members of, 120, 121
Pasmula Mahā Thera, 32
paṭipatti, 26
paṭivedha, 26
People's Liberation Front, *see* Janatā Vimukti Peramuṇa
Pērādeṇiya, 55
Percival, Robert, 69, 158
Perera, S. G. (Father), 157, 158
Perry, Edmund F., xi, xvii
peyyavajja, 5
Philippines, 110
Phybus, 63
pirit, 91, 95, 97
pirivenas, 94, 96, 106, 107, 131
  education limited, 95
  services rendered by, 95
Pirivena Teachers' Training College, 105, 110
Piyaṅgu, 21
Piyaratana Tissa, Doḍandūvē, 93, 94
points, ten, raised by the Vajji *bhikkhus,* 13
politics (*deśapālana*):
  according to Buddhism, 122 f.
  its connotation, 120
  and *nāyaka theras,* 127
  a *nāyaka thera*'s opinion on, 121, 122
  and religion, 122 f.
  and rural reconstruction, 128
  wrong opinions about *bhikkhus* and, 125 f.
Poḷonnaruva, 49, 91
Portugal, 56
Portuguese, 55, 56, 57, 58, 60, 64
Potuvila, 94
poverty, a cause of crime, 3
Prajñākīrti, Koṭahēnē, xxv, 155
Prajñāloka, Häḍipannala, xxv
Prajñārāma, Yakkaḍuvē Śrī, xxv
pratītya-samutpāda, 137
Pratyeka-Buddha, 138
Prayogaratnāvaliya, 32
Press Bill, 109
Presbyterians, 87
Prince College, xix
Protestantism, 61
Pūjāvaliya, 18, 53
Purāṇa (*bhikkhu*), 13
Puṣyamitra, 158

Qualities:
  of Benevolence, four, 122, 163
  conducive to well-being in this world, 4
  of a trader, 4

Rāhula, Walpola, xi, xii, xiii, 137, 140, 143, 162
Rājādhirājasiṃha, 23
Rājagaha, 10
Rāja Mahā Vihāra (at Kälaṇiya), 103
Rājasiṃha I, 56, 57
  his atrocities, 56
Rājasiṃha II, 58, 59, 153
Rakkhaṅga (Arakan in Lower Burma), 57. *See also* Arakan
Rāḷahāmi, 61
Ranasinghe, Sirisoma, xxvi
Rangoon, 100
Ratmalāna, 93, 105
Ratnapura, 102
Reformed Religion, 73
Refuges, Three, 21
Relics, Bowl, Hair, Tooth, of the Buddha, 19, 20
Revata, 14
Ridī Vihāra, 41
Robe-Depositor *bhikkhu,* 8
Robe-Distributor *bhikkhu,* 9
Robe-Receiving *bhikkhu,* 8
Rohaṇa, 30, 51
Roman Catholicism, 56
Roman Catholic missionaries, 56
Rome, 9
Ruhuṇa, 20, 24
Rural Reconstruction Societies (*Grāmapratisaṃskaraṇa Sabhā*), 99
Ruvanväli dāgäba, 19, 23, 25

Sabbakāmī, 14
Saddhā-Tissa (Duṭugämuṇu's brother), 20, 23

Sailabimbārāma, 93
salājeṭak, 37
samajīvikatā, 4
Saman (god Sumana), 102
samānattatā, 5
sāmaṇera, 9, 59
Samantapāsādikā (Commentary to the *Vinaya*), 6, 32, 35
Saṃgamu Vihāra, 53
saṃsāra, 3
saṃskāra, 138
Samyak-sam-Buddha, 138
sandhāna (treaty between Parākramabāhu and Gajabāhu), 52
saṅgahavatthu, 5
saṅgāyanā (at Vidyālaṅkāra Pirivena), 100
Saṅgha, 11, 12, 13, 17, 18, 20, 21, 22, 33, 39, 52, 108, 134, 135, 136 and *passim.*
  one million in the world, 109
  wealth of the, 35
  World Buddhist *Sangha* Council, 110, 137
Saṅgharakkhita Thera, 156
Sanskrit, 131
Saraṇaṅkara, Välivita Piṇḍapātika, Saṅgharāja, 32, 54, 59, 60
Sāriputta (Sāriputra, text book of art), 40
Sāsana, 26, 27, 29
Śāsanārakṣaka Samiti, 105
Satkoralē, 42
"scholarship" (*pariyatti*), 27
schools for adults, 100
Selby, H. C., 67
Sena II, 52
Senanayake, D. S., xix, xxii, 98, 164
Senkaḍagala Mahanuvara (Kandy), 76
Shaw, Bernard, 122, 124
Siam, 40, 60
Siddhārtha (Prince), 48
Siddhārtha, Hapugoḍa, xxiii
Siddhārtha, Valānē Śrī, 93
Sigāla-sutta, 5
Sīgiriya, 51
sīla, 6
Singapore, 110
Sinhala, 61, 131, and *passim.*
Sinhala Constitution, 54
Sinhala Jātika Saṅgamaya (Sinhala National Congress), 102, 103
Sinhala Kingdom, 82
Sinhala law, 18
Sinhala, medium of instruction at Vidyodaya and Vidyālaṅkāra Universities, 112
Sinhala people, their belief that the throne of Ceylon legally belonged only to a Buddhist, p. 17 f.
Sinhala, as the State language of Ceylon, 103, 104
Siri Saṅgabō (Siri Saṅghabodhi), 156
Situlpavva, 30
Sixth Council (*chaṭṭha saṅgāyanā*) in Rangoon, 100
Skanda, 102
Sobhita, Koratoṭa Śrī, 94
society, its well-being, 5
Sorata, Pim̆burē, xvii, 110
Soulbury Constitution, 164
Soviet Union, 116
śrama-dāna, 108
śrāvaka, 138
Śrī Kalyāṇi Rāja Mahā Vihāra, 136
Śrī Laṅkā, 118, 134, 135, 136, *see also* Laṅkā *and* Ceylon
Śrī Laṅkā Freedom Party (S.L.F.P.), 104, 109, 113, 114
Śrī Laṅkā Vidyālaya, 102
Śrī Vijaya Rājasiṃha, 152
Śrī Vikramarājasiṃha, 23
Stanley, Lord (Secretary of State for the Colonies), 80
Store-Keeper *bhikkhu,* 9
Subhūti, Battaramullē Śrī, 93, 94
Sumana, *see* Saman
Sumaṅgala, Hikkaḍuvē Śrī, 93, 94
Sumedha (Bodhisattva), 3, 126
Sunetrā, Queen, 53
Suttas, 42, 91
Sutta Piṭaka, 30, 31
Svastika Press, xxvi

Tamil, 18, 19, 24, 50, 55, 61
tapa, 6
Temple of the Tooth, 159
Tennent, Sir James Emerson, 155
Thailand, 101, 107, 110
Theraputtābhaya, 21
Theras (Elders), the sect of the, 14
Theravāda, 110, 137
Thullatthana, 23
Thūpārāma, 23, 52
Tibet, 109
Tipiṭaka, 3, 25, 26, 27, 29, 30, 31, 42, 96, 100, 106
Tirinanxes (*terunnānsēs*), 69, 70

Tissa, Brahmin, 24
Tissa (Mahā-Tissa), Thera, 25
Tissamahārāma, 102
Torrington, Viscount (Governor), 67, 76, 78, 80
Trainikāyika Saṅgha Sabhā, 109
Trincomalee, 58, 63
Triple Gem, 18

udakukkhepasīma, 57
Udaya III, 52
Uḍugampola, 55
Union Jack, 65
United Arab Republic, 116
United Left Front, 114, 118
United National Party (U.N.P.), 104, 109, 113
United States, 116
University of Ceylon, 100, 111
University of London, *see* London University
Upāli Mahā Thera (from Siam), 60
upasampadā, 9

Vajji *bhikkhus,* 13, 14
  ten points raised by, 13
Vaḷagambā (Vaṭṭagāmaṇī-Abhaya), 24, 25
Vanni (provinces), 55
Vanniyars, 55
Vāriyapola Thera, Vinayācārya Dīpaṃkara, 65, 157
Vasabha, queen of King, 32
vasag, 30
Vasala-sutta, 5
Vaṭṭagāmaṇī-Abhaya, *see* Vaḷagambā
vedarālas, 69
Vesāli, 13
Vibhaṅga, Commentary to, 27
Vīdāgama vihāra, 53
Vidyālaṅkāra Declaration, xx
Vidyālaṅkāra Pirivena, xvi, xix, xxiii, 42, 93, 100, 107, 133
  university status granted, 107, 112
Vidyālaṅkāra University, xviii, 161
Vidyodaya Pirivena, 93
  university status granted, 107, 112
Vidyodaya University, xvii, 137, 161
Vidyodaya and Vidyālaṅkāra Universities:
  their far-reaching effects on social and political life, 110 f.
  converted to prison camps, 117
Vietnam, 110; North Vietnam, 114
vihāra, 41, 42
Vihāra and *dēvāla* lands, Commissioners' Report, 68
Vijayabāhu I, 23, 52
Vijayabāhu IV (Bōsat Vijayabāhu), 53
Vijayasena, Kōdāgoḍa, xxiii
Vimala, Kirulaponē, 102
Vimaladharma I, 57
Vimaladharmasūrya II, 59
Vinaya, xxv, 9, 10, 13, 14, 40, 131, 132
Vinaya Piṭaka, 8, 11, 14, 30, 31, 32, 33
  Commentary to, 31
vipassanā, 26
vipassanā-dhura, 29, 30
Vipulasāra, Māpalagama, xvii, 105, 155
Vīraparākramabāhu VIII, 55
viyadam paḍiya, 38
viyāraṇ, 17

Wäligama, 56
Wesleyans, 87
Wickramasinghe, Martin, 156
Wijayasurendra, K. P. G., xvii
Wilberforce, William, 86
Wilkes, John, 120, 121
Wimaladhamma, Palannoruvē, xx
Windham, William, 74
World Buddhist *Saṅgha* Council, *see Saṅgha*
World Fellowship of Buddhists (inaugurated), 100

yakkhas, 18
Yasa, 14
Yogārṇava, 32
yojana, 36
Yugoslavia, 116